the
HIGHLANDS
&
ISLANDS
of
SCOTLAND

the HIGHLANDS & ISLANDS of SCOTLAND

ALLAN CAMPBELL McLEAN

CRESCENT BOOKS
NEW YORK

The Publishers wish to thank the following for their permission to reproduce photographs:

The front cover is Stac Polly and Cul Beag by George Young
and the back cover is Glen Etive by David MacAlpine.

Aerofilms Library 48/9 left
Bill Angus 68*
Ian Atkinson 45*
R. Balharry 79 top right
British Aluminium 64 top
British Waterways 8/9
M. Brooke 142*, 146*
Calder, McKie Associates Ltd. 89*, 92* bottom
A. Cameron 41 right
John Cleare 50, 54/5
Kenneth Cole Ltd. 49 right
Colour Library International 70, 110
Douglas Corrance 64 bottom
Dennis Coutts 155*
Department of the Environment 28 bottom, 157
John Dewar 12, 13, 16, 52, 85, 101 right, 121, 132
Duke of Beaufort/Cortauld Institute 73 bottom right
May Farrow 84, 100/1 left
A. Gilpin 10 top, 149
David Gowans 51, 58 bottom right, 63, 80, 82/3, 106/7 left, 138/9 right
Grant Collection 52, 116/7, right
D. Hardley 34, 35 left and right
From *Highland Railway* by H. A. Vallance (David & Charles) 97 left
Highlands and Islands Development Board 46 left, 47,
71, 87, 111, 115 bottom right, 130, 147
H. R. Jenkins 42/3 left
David Kilpatrick 28 top, 29, 38
M. Luciani 116* left
D. MacAlpine 14/15 right, 138 bottom left
Sir Robert McAlpine Ltd. 25 right
A. D. S. MacPherson 17 top, 24/5 left, 36/7, 56/7, 61,
108/9 right, 124/5 left, 128 bottom, 129, 136/7
Oscar Marzaroli 46 bottom right, 53, 58 left, 58/9 right,
72/3 left, 81, 126, 127 left, 134, 135, 140 left,
141, 147 left, 152, 153 left and right
R. Mattassa 62
C. K. Mylne 79 bottom right
National Trust for Scotland 44, 69
North of Scotland Hydro Electric Board 37 top and bottom
Ogam Films 96*, 113*, 125* right, 133*, 140 right, 143*, 156*
David Paterson 30*, 66*, 67*, 76/7, 86, 90*, 91, 98, 102 bottom, 104/5, 108 left, 131
A. Paton 43* right
R. J. Pearce 10 bottom, 39, 78/9 left
Edith Pennie 103 top
Ian Pennie 102 top left, 103 bottom left, 107 right
Photoval 93* right
W. Ralston 25
Scottish National Portrait Gallery 73 top, 93 left, 128 top
Jack Selby 114, 115 top and bottom left
Sherriff's Bowmore 17 bottom left and right
D. Sim 99
M. Singleton 138 top left
Sutherland Estates 97 right
Eric Thorburn 31*, 33*, 40/1* left, 144* left and right, 145*, 148*
Bobby Tulloch 150, 151
Andrew Watson 92 top
Waverley Steam Navigation Co. Ltd. 21
Gus Wylie 118, 119, 122 left and right, 123, 127 right
George Young 7*, 11*, 14* left, 18, 19 left and right, 22*,
23* left and right, 26, 27*, 74*, 75*, 95*, 102* top right,
103* bottom right, 112*, 154* top and bottom

*Asterisk denotes Highlands and Islands Development Board Copyright

CONTENTS

This book was produced in co-operation with
The Highlands and Islands Development Board
which is a unique agency set up by Parliament in
1965 to encourage and promote the economic and
social development of Scotland's seven Highland
counties – Zetland, Orkney, Caithness,
Sutherland, Ross-shire, Inverness-shire and Argyll.

MID ARGYLL
KINTYRE
GIGHA AND ISLAY

Kintyre.

PASSAGE OF HER MAJESTY ON THE CRINAN CANAL.

Queen Victoria's sumptuously decorated barge on a royal progression through the Crinan Canal in 1847. The Queen was embarked on a tour of the Western Isles. Had the monarch any inkling of the ferocious weather that awaited her in the storm-swept Minch she would have made a smart about-turn at Crinan and never left the calm of the canal. Significantly, there were no more royal cruises to the Hebrides. Balmoral became the safely landlocked Highland seat of the Royal family.

Kintyre is the longest peninsula in Scotland, thrusting south west like a great longboat hungry for the haven of the blue hills of Antrim. It is not so fanciful a notion; the lighthouse at the Mull of Kintyre casts its beam across a mere twelve miles of sea to the coast of Ireland.

Scottish history sparked to life here. This is ancient Dalriada, first Kingdom of the Scots. The fishing port of Campbeltown on the south-east coast stands on the site of the old capital of Dalruadhain. An aura of its regal past still lingers. The imperious sweep of the broad bay has a certain hauteur hardly in keeping with the modest presence of a little market town.

But Campbeltown, intimately linked with the countryside of Kintyre, needs no capital status to be conscious of its importance. Within the sea-girt boundaries of Kintyre, Campbeltown is king, and no small town in all Scotland inspires fiercer loyalties. Expatriate Campbeltonians, no matter how spectacular their success in the wider world, rarely lose touch with the town of their birth. For exiles intent upon a more active return than a retirement pilgrimage, the homeward road has become a much more practical proposition.

The singular characteristics of the broad bay on Campbeltown Loch that drew the first Scots to the heel of the long peninsula have a contemporary relevance. As the oil-extraction industry moves west and into the Celtic Sea, Campbeltown acquires ever greater significance on the maps of the oil-men.

As a fishing port, it had the distinction of being the site of Scotland's newest shipyard, builders of the first steel fishing boat to be launched in Highland waters. Those waters are the source of new wealth from below the sea-bed, and a burgeoning Campbeltown has been fired by a fresh dynamism.

Across from Campbeltown on the west coast lies Machrihanish, known to golfers the world over. Few courses can claim Atlantic-washed links and a conveniently adjacent airport.

For the motorist and walker alike, one of the delights of Kintyre's coast roads is the exhilarating seascapes – richly patterned by islands – that are rarely out of sight. On the west, the clustering tail of the Southern Hebrides can be seen. Tiny Gigha, unlikely harbourer of the luxuriant oasis of Achamore Garden; Jura of the illustrious Paps, and the Green Isle of Islay.

The east coast road, along the length of Kilbrannan Sound, opens new windows on the majestic mountains of Arran, authentically Highland in their grandeur. Whilst to the south, the absurdly theatrical back-cloth of Ailsa Craig – rising sheer out of the firth – rivets the eye.

The fishing village of Tarbert links Kintyre and Knapdale on the wrist-thin isthmus between the long sea-loch of West Loch Tarbert and the inlet of East Loch Tarbert on Loch Fyne. Magnus Barefoot, King of Norway, had his war-galley hauled across the isthmus in the year 1093. A classic case of brute strength being harnessed to an imaginative ploy in psychological warfare. Native watchers in the heather who survived the shock of a Viking war-galley moving on land must have been unmanned thereafter.

Tarbert sits in an idyllic picture post-card frame; a superb harbour crowded with inshore fishing boats, the occasional yacht and pleasure cruiser looking a trifle self-conscious in such uncompromisingly workaday company.

In the eighteenth century, plans were mooted for a canal across the narrow isthmus to eliminate the long sail around the Mull of Kintyre to the Atlantic Ocean. But Sir John Rennie's design for a canal linking Loch Gilp and Loch Crinan gained favour, and the earlier scheme was abandoned. Work started on Sir John's nine miles-long Crinan Canal in 1793, and it was opened to shipping in 1801.

In 1847, Queen Victoria made a royal progression through the canal on her way to the Western Isles.

The Queen's sumptuously decorated barge was drawn by three horses, guided by postillions arrayed in scarlet. Whilst not quite so awe-inspiring as the crossing of Magnus Barefoot 750 years earlier, it was certainly a passage fit for a Queen Empress. The natives were suitably impressed.

Alas, such glories are no more. Nowadays, the canal is used by the Loch Fyne fishing fleet taking mundane passage to the northern fishing grounds. Only faint echoes of that majestic progress are aroused when lissom thoroughbreds of yachts, bound for a summer cruise of the Western Isles, ease their sleek flanks through the fifteen locks.

At Crinan, on the Sound of Jura, the sea is carpeted with islands. Crinan looks out on the Dorus Mor, the Great Door, between Craignish Point and the island of Garbh Reisa. This is the sea-gateway to the Isles of the Hebrides; a gateway guarded by an all too realistic sea-dragon – the roaring whirlpool of Corryvrechan.

The Gulf of Corryvrechan lies between the islands of Jura and Scarba. The flood-tide storms west through the gulf at a furious nine

Opposite bottom. Tarbert – with the photogenic ruins of
a fourteenth-century castle obligingly perched on the
shore – sits in an idyllic picture postcard frame. These
sheltered waters once harboured the war-galley of
Magnus Barefoot, King of Norway. Nowadays, there
are only summer invaders – sleek yachts and pleasure
cruisers, mingling a little self-consciously with the
workaday boats of the Loch Fyne herring fleet.

Opposite top. The grandeur of Loch Fyne – which has
given its name to one of the delights of the Scottish
table, the Loch Fyne kipper.

Above. Inveraray Castle, conceived on a truly ducal
scale by Archibald, 3rd Duke of Argyll and Lord Justice
General of Scotland. Fire destroyed the roof of the
castle in November 1975.

11

knots, smashing against underwater peaks. The upsurge creates a fearsome whirlpool, which has been the graveyard of countless vessels over the centuries. When a westerly wind blows against the tide-race, the roar of the whirlpool can be heard on the Knapdale coast.

Inveraray, at the head of Loch Fyne, is synonymous with the Earls of Argyll, any one of whom – in their medieval heyday – would have given Cesare Borgia a run for his Lira.

Seeing Inveraray today, drowsing on a tranquil headland between the River Aray and the tiny stream of the Cromalt, it requires a conscious effort of imagination to visualize its savage past. It seems incongruous that such a sedate little town – keeping its decorous distance from the regal magnificence of Inveraray Castle – could have known fire, sword and carnage.

But Inveraray's history was forged in far from sedate times. Fire, sword and carnage it knew to its bitter cost, tied as it was to the fluctuating fortunes of its Campbell grandees. The town's present ordered state stems from the organizing ability of one man – Archibald, 3rd Duke of Argyll and Lord Justice General of Scotland.

Succeeding to the title at the age of 61, and returning to Inveraray for the first time since the rebellion of 1715, he engaged the London architect Roger Morris – with William Adam as his Man Friday on the spot – to supervise the building of a new castle. As the rude huts of his clansmen impaired the landscaping of the castle grounds, Duke Archibald conceived a truly ducal solution; he would lay out a new town.

On his death, his son John took over. The saga of Campbell reconstruction continued with the 5th duke, who completed the new town of Inveraray and refurbished the interior of the castle.

What was once the domain of one of the great notables of the land, is now open daily to the public from April to October. Not least among the castle treasures is a magnificent bronze cannon – salvaged from the sunken Spanish galleon in Tobermory Bay – bearing the arms of Francis 1 of France. The old kitchen is preserved as it was a century ago; a singular monument to the heroic labours of the domestics of the period.

Perhaps the best monuments of all are to be found in the grounds; noble trees, some of them planted by distinguished hands. William

Ewart Gladstone and Alfred, Lord Tennyson did their stint. So did that indefatigable planter of trees, the extraordinary ex-Empress Eugenie of France, whose incredibly long life spanned the founding of the Kingdom of Greece in 1827 and the first direct flight across the Atlantic in 1919.

Of all Kintyre's clustering flotilla of islands, tiny Gigha is the closest to the mainland, only three miles from Tayinloan.

The Gulf Stream makes it ideal dairying country, and milk production from the island's Ayrshire cattle is of the order of 300,000 gallons a year. The milk is collected from the modernized farm byres – each with its own cooling tank – by bulk tanker, and transported to the Gigha Creamery where the skilled cheese-makers take over.

One of Gigha's great strengths is that its population, although microscopic by urban standards, forms a socially cohesive whole, being happily free of the age imbalance which is the scourge of so many Hebridean islands. All of them take pride in the fact that their island is the home of one of Scotland's great gardens; a garden brought to full fruition by the late Sir James Horlick in an astonishingly brief span of years.

Opposite. In 1801 Sir John Rennie's nine miles-long Crinan Canal, linking Loch Gilp and Loch Crinan, was opened to shipping, enabling vessels to avoid the long sail around the Mull of Kintyre to the Atlantic Ocean. One of the gems of Mid Argyll, the canal is a rare instance of the works of man achieving a perfect accord with nature. As urban man seeks respite from the increasingly frenetic round of city life, the chances are that this quiet waterway will enjoy a new lease of life of a kind that its creator could hardly have foreseen.

Above. There is a cosy, workaday domesticity about Tarbert when the fishing boats crowd the jetty.

13

Above. Loch Fyne, one of the longest sea lochs in Scotland; the historic sea road to the heart of Argyll.

Opposite. Port Charlotte, Queen of the Rhinns of Islay, untouched by the abrasive twentieth century. In Sraid Ard the pavement on the left is walled and raised above the road level, whilst that on the right is walled and set below the road level. It is a typically civilized Islay solution to the problem of separating pedestrian and traffic.

Sir James became the Laird of Gigha in 1944, and created Achamore Garden from an original mixed woodland planted at the turn of the century to provide cover for game. The woodland now provides shelter for 50 acres of superlative garden.

From the seat on the hill above Achamore, the mainland coast of Kintyre, the dominating Paps of Jura, Islay and the distant hills of Ireland are all within view. Cath Sgeir and Dubh Sgeir, Gigha's bare inshore reefs, poke spiky fingers out to sea. Inland, there are fertile green meadows, browsing cattle, a scatter of farmhouses and steadings; a common enough pastoral scene. But plunge down the steep, overgrown path through the steamy jungle of the woods, and another world bursts upon the eye. It is a catalogue of colour.

The great spread of the Rhododendron Falconeri, over 20 feet wide, bearing immense creamy-yellow trusses. Its cinnamon coloured trunk and branches have a curiously polished, sculpted finish, oddly sensuous.

The pinks, reds and whites of the azaleas on the Farm Road, draping the hillside in sheets of varying hue.

Orange, light yellow and white azaleas in the North Drive.

Flame trees, glowing orange-scarlet, at their dazzling best in May and June.

The Hospital Garden, protected by a 15-feet high, wafer-thin hedge – thickly clothed to the ground although a mere 18 inches in width – leading on to the magnificence of the Sino Grande Tree Fern with its backing of rhododendrons.

The great arch of twin cyprus – 35–feet high – opening into a flowered glade.

The mannered elegance of the Pond Garden; an exotic interloper on a Hebridean island.

Above all, those most famous of all rhododendrons, flaunting their blossoms in riotous profusion, the Horlick hybrids.

In 1962, Sir James gave the plant collection of the garden, together with an endowment for its future maintenance, to the National Trust for Scotland. In a very personal sense, Achamore Garden is his living memorial. He was a great gardener, and his garden – open to the public from 1st April to 30th September – must rank as one of the wonders of the West.

Islay, the most southerly of the Inner Hebrides, is only a brief flight from London but light-years removed from the Great Wen in scene and tempo. No island has a more diverse variety of bird habitat; woodland, moor, hill, sea-cliff, machair, sand-dune, agricultural land, river, marsh, freshwater loch, and the two great sea-lochs of Indaal and Gruinart.

The island is one of the world's major wintering resorts of the barnacle goose – over 8000 at a recent count, more than double Islay's human population – and grey-lags and Greenland whitefronts are regular visitors.

All islands should be savoured at leisure, but the tranquil aura of Islay is so pervasive that even those tied to a tight timetable must be tempted to make a quiet bonfire of their itinerary and let their days on Islay drift into weeks.

Port Charlotte, Queen of the Rhinns of Islay, demands time to stand and stare.

Linger on the delicate symmetry of the crescent line of marching chimney pots on the terrace row of Bruthach Dubh. Sleek, slated roofs cap colour-washed walls, gay with painted windowsills. A peat stack, artfully arranged against the gable wall of the end house, adds an aesthetically pleasing but essentially practical island flavour.

Stroll along Sraid Ard Street; the pavement on the left walled and raised *above* the road

15

level; that on the right walled and set *below* the road level. It sounds crazy, but it works; a civilized separation of pedestrian and traffic.

The essence of Port Charlotte is the archway near the bottom of Cnoc Iain Phail, opening on to an inner court revealing Loch Indaal and the sea beyond. Listen to the rumble of shingle into the rocky gullies fronting the houses; a heart-beat of quiet, and then the tinny rattle of the ebb.

Then there is dreamy Bridgend of the welcoming little hotel, with the River Sorn flowing through lush meadows and wooded flats. The Bank of Scotland – built on the river bank in 1838 – so charmingly situated it must be a delight to have an overdraft there.

Ducks abounding in Loch Indaal, scaup,

merganser and golden-eye, busily cavorting around the pier at Bowmore. An incongruously wide street – fit to swallow a juggernaut – cleaves arrow-straight from the pier to the droll, circular church, reputedly of that shape to prevent the Devil hiding in corners.

Blue seas creaming on black rocks east of Port Ellen, with the pagoda-like roofs of famous distilleries – Laphroaig, Lagavulin, Ardbeg – in the distance.

The bleak, bare snout of The Oa peninsula, peopled by the ghosts of hunted smugglers.

A critical gallery of black guillemots on the cliff above Port Askaig, surveying the departing steamer with ill-concealed disdain. Who could blame them for wanting to keep the Green Isle of Islay to themselves?

Opposite. The roaring whirlpool of Corryvrechan between the islands of Jura and Scarba. When a westerly wind blows against the tide-race the roar of the whirlpool can be heard on the Knapdale coast.

Top. A street fit for juggernauts cleaves arrow-straight from the pier to Bowmore's droll, circular church. The church was so designed to prevent the Devil hiding in corners; a foul slander on the eagle-eyed elders of the day, who were forever discovering the Devil in darker places than corners.

Above right. Starting the magical mix on the malting floor.

Above left. The pagoda-like roofs of famous distilleries.

DUNOON AND COWAL

Opposite. Yachtsmen have always come to the Firth of Clyde to savour the joys of a heaving deck and a good breeze of wind off Cowal.

Above. The 'heavies' at the Cowal Games. Stripped down to vest and kilt, stepping lightly for all their bulk, the big fellows have a rare swagger on them, lordly as a pride of lions.

The history of Dunoon as a holiday resort can be traced back to its inauspicious start in the year 1779. An enterprising Glasgow family by the name of Reid decided to spend the summer in the then virtually unknown clachan on the south-east coast of Cowal. They embarked at the Broomielaw on their voyage of discovery.

The trip down the Clyde and across the Firth was not without its hazards. Their hired wherry – overladen with a sufficiency of supplies to carry the provident Reids through the summer – stuck fast on a sandbank.

It was a classic situation for a scurrilous lampoon. The Reids were in imminent danger of being immortalized in a folk ballad under the all too obvious title of *'The Glesga Gluttons.'* Nothing daunted, they promptly issued a statement pointing out the reason for the excessive weight of a cargo destined for their own stomachs. They could, one of the party explained with engaging candour, *'put no dependence on getting provisions, not even fish, in such an out of the way place.'*

The wherry eventually floated clear on the flood-tide, but a safe landfall at Dunoon posed yet another problem for the pioneering Reids. To their dismay, they discovered that the local minister was the only inhabitant who spoke English.

It is not recorded if the Reid family stayed long enough to acquire a full understanding of the theological subtleties contained in the minister's Gaelic sermons, but there was certainly a prolonged hiatus in the development of Dunoon as a holiday centre. Fate was busy hatching a catalyst. It came in the unlikely guise of a brilliant young engineer, Henry Bell.

Once Bell's steamship, the *Comet*, had survived the considerable perils of her maiden voyage down the Clyde in 1822, the technological revolution in sea transport was safely under way. It led to the era of the Clyde steamer, as great a liberating influence in its day as Henry Ford's Model 'T' in the early decades of this century.

The lure of cheap transport galvanized Glasgow's static industrial workers, cooped in their grim sandstone tenements. They streamed 'doon the watter' in their thousands to the green coast of Cowal. It was an open playground close enough to the heart of the industrial wasteland for them to regard it as their own backyard; a clean, sea-washed backyard unscathed by the grimy, ravaging monster that the industrial revolution had unleashed to despoil the Clyde Valley.

Entrepreneurs, like Robert Hunter of Hatton who was acute enough to acquire a large chunk of the coast before the steamer-boom transformed the holiday habits of the masses, were waiting to welcome them. The holiday resort of Dunoon was born.

Although it has played host to millions over the years, Dunoon is no more than an urban bridgehead on the hilly coast of Cowal. The interior has not greatly changed from the days when the Stewart kings hunted wild boar, and the Campbells of Loch Fyne herded their black cattle along the drove road through Hell's Glen to Lochgoilhead and the markets of the south.

From its mountainous northern neck, the peninsula of Cowal is bounded in the west by the embracing arm of Loch Fyne and in the east by Loch Long and the broad waters of the Firth of Clyde. The Isle of Bute thrusts a thumb into the crab-like claws of the southern seaboard, forming the Kyles of Bute, the

favourite seaway of the Clyde steamers.

The deeply indented southern coast strengthens the impression – fostered by the shuttling car-ferry from Gourock to Dunoon – that Cowal, like Bute, is an island. But there is a land route to Cowal, one that offers the traveller from the south the bonus of a sudden, dramatic change in the landscape and an early confrontation with the West Highland scene.

From Arrochar the road winds through Glen Croe to the summit of Rest and Be Thankful at the western end of the glen. A road sweeps down through Gleann Mor from the summit of the pass to the head of Loch Goil on the east coast.

Bare facts often conceal the whole truth. To describe Loch Goil as a branch of Loch Long is factually correct, but grossly misleading in that it conveys an impression of secondary status, whereas Loch Goil of the high hills is the peer of all the lovely lochs of Cowal.

The village of Lochgoilhead, grouped around the head of the loch, is notable for the antiquity of its church which dates from the fifteenth century. This is Campbell country, the lineage indelibly marked in the churchyard where the Campbells of Ardkinglas have buried their dead for six centuries.

The brooding heron can be seen fishing patiently off the shores of Loch Goil, and schools of cavorting porpoise – scorning the heron's staid approach to his craft – have been known to hunt the herring shoals up the loch. The surrounding hills are the haunt of the golden eagle and peregrine falcon, and wild cat still lurk in the lonely corries.

North through Hell's Glen, the road through the pass offers views of Inveraray on

Once Henry's steamship, the *Comet*, had survived the considerable perils of her maiden voyage down the Clyde in 1812, the technological revolution in sea transport was safely under way. It led to the era of the Clyde steamer, as great a liberating influence in its day as Henry Ford's Model 'T' in the early decades of this century. Last in the line of the elegant old paddle-steamers, the *Waverley* epitomizes a vanished era.

the west side of Loch Fyne. Seen from the heights across the loch, the ancient stronghold of the Campbells of Argyll has an idyllic air grotesquely at odds with the life-style of the Campbell chiefs, whose power was only temporarily eclipsed by the loss of the ninth earl's head to the executioner's axe.

A few miles south of the old ferry crossing from St Catherines to Inveraray, the hills of Cowal are cleft by a long glen stretching from Strachur to Dunoon. Loch Eck, the biggest freshwater loch in Cowal, lies midway between the two.

The road south follows the shoreline of Loch Fyne as far as Otter Ferry and reaches

down to Ardlamont, the heartland of clan Lamont. The rule of the Lamonts in south Cowal clashed with Campbell ambitions and ferocious tribal vendettas soaked the land in blood.

The east branch of the crossroads at Millhouse leads to Kames and Tighnabruaich on the Kyles of Bute. Tighnabruaich has succeeded in retaining its Highland character. Sheltered by hills and trees, with the narrow moat of the Kyle separating it from the green hills of Bute, no village could be better fitted for the role of tranquil backwater. One of the delights of Tighnabruaich lies off-shore; its attendant cluster of yachts, bright and silent

Opposite. The land route to Cowal winds through Glen Croe, dominated by the distinctive peak of The Cobbler, to the summit of Rest and Be Thankful.

Above left. The River Goil flows into Loch Goil, peer of all the famed sea-lochs of Cowal.

Above right. The River Ruel meanders through the tranquil green heart of Cowal, so close to the industrial wasteland but so miraculously unscathed.

as butterflies, fitting consorts for a village with no grandiose ambitions.

Benmore Gardens provide another welcome retreat. These woodland gardens extend from the River Eachaig to Glen Massan south of Loch Eck, and were gifted to the nation by Mr H. G. Younger in 1925. Under the enlightened administration of the Royal Botanic Gardens of Edinburgh, a comprehensive collection of rhododendrons has been established at Benmore. More than 200 species are represented, as well as many rare trees and plants from abroad. In the woods to the north, there is a pond of spectacular golden carp. But the most magnificent sight of all is the main avenue of redwoods, dignified giants towering more than a hundred feet high.

The outflow of Loch Eck runs into the Holy Loch, the base for the depot ship of the American *Polaris* squadron. God must have a sardonic sense of humour, as a Highland wag once remarked when commenting on this unholy alliance.

The village of Kilmun on the shores of the Holy Loch derives its name from Saint Mun, a contemporary of Saint Columba. The gentle Saint Mun founded the monastery of Kilmun in the seventh century. In 1442, Sir Duncan Campbell – doubtless influenced by the sanctity of the site – in turn founded a collegiate church there. His church did not survive the gross excesses of the Scottish Reformation, but the domed mausoleum of the Campbells of Argyll has endured. To this day Kilmun remains the burial place of the chiefs of clan Campbell.

Sandbank has featured in more recent history. It is the site of the most famous yacht-yard in Cowal, birthplace of those American Cup challengers of nostalgic memory, *Sceptre* and *Sovereign*.

From Sandbank, the coast road to Dunoon goes out by Lazaretto Point, once a quarantine station, described a century and a half ago as, *'the place where vessels loaded with cotton discharge their cargoes and perform quarantine.'* The Lazaretto is no more than a memory, like the past glories of Hunters Quay, once the focal point of the great Clyde regattas that attracted yachts and yachtsmen from every part of the country.

Dunoon crowds around a double bay – East Bay and West Bay – divided by the headland of Castle Hill. The royal castle of Dunoon belonged originally to the hereditary high-stewards of Scotland to whom King Malcolm

— with typical monarchial largesse – gave a grant of Bute and Cowal in the eleventh century. All that remains of the historic fortress, once the jealously prized possession of the Earls of Argyll, are a few scattered stones on the grassy crown of Castle Hill. The castle was totally destroyed by the rampaging Murray of Atholl in 1685. It was a suitably ignominious end for the mute witness of the slaughter of the Lamonts by the Campbells; a massacre notable – even by the permissive standards of the seventeenth century – for its grisly blend of treacherous savagery.

The famous pier on the point was built by the famous Stevensons – father and uncle of the immortal Robert Louis – and its period character has in no way been impaired by the later reconstruction. The pier belongs to the era of the paddle-steamer, as do the miles of promenade lined by solid Victorian villas, once the homes of wealthy Glasgow merchants who had achieved the supreme status symbol of a house on the coast. The villas are now private hotels and guest houses, as unequivocally Scottish in their aura of formal rectitude as the high teas served within their substantial walls.

Nostalgia is a Scottish trait which is one

Opposite. The mountains of Arran from the Kyles of Bute, those scenic straits that became synonymous with the Clyde steamer traffic.

Above. The curious juxtaposition of the verdant tip of the Cowal peninsula and the oil-production platform yard at Ardyne Point. Descendants of those workers who first made the trip 'doon the watter' on a brief annual escape from the stifling bondage of their industrial prison now commute daily to Ardyne – to work.

25

of the reasons why cheap package tours to the Costa Brava have not wiped Dunoon off the tourist map. There is a peculiarly Scottish homeliness about the place, evoking memories of innocent pleasures in simpler days when the sun always shone and instant fulfilment was to be found in an ice-cream cone or a bottle of fizzy lemonade.

The scenes at the end of the Cowal Highland Games – the supreme annual event of the summer season – are laden with nostalgia. The pipe bands march back from the sports stadium into the town bearing their trophies through the crowded streets. Fathers hoist their sons shoulder-high for a better view, just as they were once lifted on high as small boys to see the march past of the kilted giants.

But paradoxes abound. A short drive south from Dunoon leads to Ardyne Point, fenced by a tracery of tall derricks. An army of construction workers is engaged here building concrete production platforms for oil-fields in the deep waters east of Shetland. Many of them come from Glasgow and Paisley and Clydebank, descendants of those workers who first made the trip 'doon the watter' in transitory flight from their grim industrial bondage. None of them could have foreseen that their children's children would one day journey to Ardyne Point, on the tip of the Cowal Peninsula, to earn their daily bread.

OBAN, MULL AREA

Opposite. The distant ramparts of Arran. Above. Oban.

Above. Even the harsh angularity of Connel Bridge, spanning the Etive narrows, is softened in the milky western light.

Below. The old furnace of Lorn, justly recognised as an industrial monument worthy of preservation.

Opposite. Castle Stalker, home of the Stewarts of Appin, stands four-square on its tiny islet of green at the mouth of Loch Laich.

Oban is beyond compare in the splendour of its approaches. All the superbly scenic roads of Lorn converge upon the town.

The meandering coast road from the south plays hide and seek with the Firth of Lorn; a firth richly patterned with islands and crowding shoals of skerries and reefs. Their names sound like an incantation to old, forgotten gods.

Scarba and Lunga; the close-flanked western scimitar of the Isles of the Sea – Eileach an Naoimh, A' Chuli, Garbh Eileach and Dun Chonnuill – Shuna, Luing and Torsa filling the broad mouth of Loch Melfort; and that long stepping stone to the mainland, Seil.

Clachan Bridge – inevitably given the touristy tag of 'The Bridge Across The Atlantic' – spans Clachan Sound linking the Isle of Seil to the mainland. Designed by Thomas Telford – whose lasting imprint upon the Highland scene constitutes a remarkable memorial to a long life of incredibly sustained creative energy – the bridge's single stone arch rises steeply above the sound, enabling small vessels to pass below at high tide.

The road from the north swings down through historic Appin along the placid shores of Loch Linnhe. Close to Portnacroish, on a

green-topped islet in the inlet of Loch Laich, stands the ancient seat of the Stewarts of Appin. It is Castle Stalker, surely the most attractive castle in all Scotland.

Standing proudly four-square on its tiny islet of green, ringed by the blue waters of the loch, the little castle looks out on a backdrop of the Morvern Hills rising high above the long thin finger of Lismore.

Seen in the brilliant early-morning light of a glittering summer day, with a flat calm on the loch carrying a three-dimensional mirror image of the Castle of the Hunter, even the most avaricious property speculator would be tempted to abandon his city fortress for a site such as this.

Built in the thirteenth century, the castle was refurbished in 1450 by Duncan Stewart of Appin as a hunting lodge for James IV, and in the course of its long history it has been the focal point of infinitely more deadly pursuits. But it has a curiously innocent, domesticated air, enhanced by the outside stone stairway leading to the gateway on the first floor. Not that any medieval visitant would have failed to observe the bulging parapet on the battlements above the entrance, carefully holed so that boiling oil or pitch could be accurately directed on the heads of unwanted guests.

From the east, the road to Oban skirts Loch Awe under the dominant peak of Ben Cruachan. Cruachan is the hollow mountain, heart of the hydro-electric pumped-storage scheme. It is an impressive example of the way in which natural forces can be harnessed without despoiling the landscape.

The only visible signs of the colossal engineering exertions which have gone on here are the screened, curving intake on the loch adjacent to the Administration Building, and the reservoir, high above Loch Awe, made by damming a natural corrie under the peak of Ben Cruachan.

An access road-tunnel penetrates two-thirds of a mile into the heart of the mountain where an enormous cavern – 300-feet long and 120-feet high – has been hacked out of solid rock to house the Machine Hall and its incumbent giants, four huge turbine/generator sets. One of the staggering statistics relating to Cruachan is the fact that the Machine Hall – big enough to swallow Coventry Cathedral with ease – is located 118 feet *below* the level of Loch Awe.

In the aseptic control room – a bewildering mass of computerized gadgetry; consoles,

Above. Portsonachan on Loch Awe; a favourite haunt of anglers drawn by the lure of the loch's sea trout.

Opposite. The curiously modernistic architecture of Balemartin, Tiree. Sunny Tiree was once the granary of Iona.

dials, arrays of buttons – it is difficult to believe that the three shirt-sleeved operators are working deep in the heart of the mountain. From such an unlikely base, they have gigantic power under fingertip control. Not only the 400 megawatt power of Cruachan, but the stations at Nant and Inverawe, and the switching stations at Dalmally and Taynuilt.

Driving out by the road-tunnel, the gleaming walls of bare rock glistening under the thin thread of overhead lights, the magnitude of this engineering feat becomes borne in upon the visitor. Acutely conscious of the weight of rock above, few sights are more satisfying than that of Loch Awe, framed in the tunnel mouth, virtually untouched by the Herculean labours that have hollowed out a mountain.

The Oban road thrusts through the Pass of Brander, scene of an attempted MacDougall ambush on The Bruce more than six centuries ago.

Along that road the little village of Taynuilt at the foot of Glen Nant furnishes a curious footnote to history, a footnote written in stone by a forgotten industrial community whose members toiled without the benefit of hydro-electric power. Behind the church of Muckairn is a monument to Lord Nelson raised in this

Highland village by a strange band of immigrants – Englishmen all.

In the sixteenth century, English woodlands were being decimated by the iron-smelters. Queen Elizabeth prohibited further felling by royal decree. The ironmasters promptly flitted to Taynuilt, importing ore and experienced workmen from the south. On news of Nelson's victory and death at Trafalgar, the patriotic English immigrants raised a standing stone, bearing the inscription;

To the memory of Lord Nelson: this stone was erected by the Lorn Furnace workmen in 1805.

A few years later, the introduction of blast furnaces put the technological boot in the old industry, and the memory of the English furnacemen of Lorn has all but perished with it. But their memorial to Nelson remains, and it was erected 37 years before a grateful government got around to commemorating the national hero in Trafalgar Square.

The old furnace of Lorn still stands on the shore of Loch Etive. It has now been justly recognized as an industrial monument worthy of preservation, and has been taken under the protective wing of the Department of the Environment.

Oban is a town graced by physical endow-ments which match the splendour of its hinterland. Ringed by wooded hills, the town has grown around a deep bay. A rocky bastion guards the bay from the north, surmounted by ivy-walled Dunollie Castle, and the southern end is protected by the Dungallon headland. The green hills of Kerrera form a natural harbour bar. Beyond Kerrera, the mountains of Mull loom above the Firth of Lorn. Roses in bloom at Christmas are a flowering proof of the town's sheltered setting.

Above the North Pier – shunned by the serried ranks of hotels lining the seafront, which steadfastly face out over the harbour, concentrating their decorous gaze on the three piers, the crowded steamers and car-ferries, weathered, workaday fishing boats, sleek yachts and busy motor launches – stands Oban's most famous monument, McCaig's Folly, a preposterous mini Colosseum.

This absurd flight of Victorian fancy – in enduring granite – was conceived by a local banker who clearly did not live in dread of directives from Head Office. John Stuart McCaig's grandiose fantasies, and his admir-able aim of assisting unemployed masons at a time of economic recession, have ensured him a dubious immortality, and lumbered Oban

31

and its citizens with a permanent problem.

The interior of the roofless round tower has now been converted into a garden. But the most imaginative stroke of all has been the bold floodlighting of McCaig's Folly; an act of pure theatre, transforming the granite monster into a wonderfully ethereal spectacle. On the credit side, McCaig's Folly does serve a useful purpose if it draws the curious – and the incredulous – up the hill for a closer look. The seaward window arches of the round tower provide one of the best vantage points of all to savour the full sweep of Oban's bay and Mull of the mountains across the Firth of Lorn.

Oban owed its explosive growth in the last century to the coming of the steamship and the railway. Summer tours to Oban, by rail and steamer from London, were widely advertised. Londoners who had qualms about venturing so far north must have been reassured by the billing. Oban was always described as 'The Charing Cross Of The Highlands.'

But the advent of the railway in 1880 came close to destroying the town's greatest asset. The deep crescent of Oban's bay lay between the site of the proposed railway terminus and the North Pier. The railway company planned to run their line across the bay from the south shore to the pier on an embankment; an act of vandalism that would have destroyed the outlook from the town.

Those opposed to the embankment wanted the railway limited to the south shore, or tucked away in Lochavullin at the back of the town. The rival factions each had their own press support. The *Oban Telegraph* was pro-, the *Oban Times* anti-embankment. It is perhaps significant that of the two rival newspapers it is the *Oban Times* that has survived to the

The long, thin finger of Loch Etive, poking deep into the hills of the Blackmount Forest.

Above. The road through Benderloch, one of the superbly scenic roads of Lorn.

Opposite left. Majestic Loch Awe, the magnificent south-east frontier of Lorn.

Opposite right. A tangle of sheep make the crossing from Lismore to Oban market.

present day; the *Telegraph* expired in 1903.

The supporters of the embankment claimed that railway and steamers must be brought together at the North Pier. Taking the war into the enemy's camp they maintained that Oban Bay, far from being a tourist attraction, was really a cesspool. The Black Lynn, which served as a channel for the town's untreated sewage, emptied into the bay in front of the main street. Letters appeared describing the Black Lynn as a *'dirty sloopy strand which gives forth both smells and sights to disgust the pure-eyed and pure-nostrilled promenaders of George Street'*, and castigating the *'filthy and offensive foreshore polluted with town sewage and every nameless abomination'*, which stank with *'the most fetid effluvium that ever frightened away a tourist.'*

It was not simply a case of some towns-folk being blessed – or cursed – with more sensitive nostrils than others. The florid prose conceals the fact that the pro-embankment lobby hoped to have the bay filled in and the sewage piped beyond the barrier of the embankment at the railway company's expense.

The *Oban Telegraph* pulled out all the stops, waxing lyrical; *'If the iron horse is to come to our coast he will come laden with valuable commodities for the public benefit, and we ought therefore to receive him in no churlish spirit. Instead of restricting him to a shed out-side our walls let us give him free access to an ornamental stable in the very heart of the burgh.'*

Dr Campbell of Ballachulish slammed back in the *Oban Times*; *'A more insane and pre-posterous scheme could hardly be conceived. It will convert our Obanian Princes Street into a Broomielaw. It would be better that Oban should never see the railway than that it should see it only to become extinct.'*

Civil war was averted by the railway company purchasing recently reclaimed land on the south side of the bay, and deciding to build its own pier alongside the station.

The news had a traumatic effect on John Stuart McCaig, owner of the North Pier. Rushing to a meeting of railway shareholders in Glasgow – and judging by his impassioned oration suitably fortified by the product of the local distillery – he denounced the new scheme as being wildly extravagant.

The reclaimed land, according to the dis-traught banker, was a stage projecting into the bay, and *'on this stage a beautiful station whose Grecian columns will be taught to support springing Roman arches full of life and vitality, a splendid sea esplanade with plate-glass verandas along the side of the station – the whole variously estimated at from £50,000 to £100,000 – will be built.'*

The modest terminal that eventually arose bore no relation to McCaig's incoherent fantasy, although the genesis of his later Folly high above the North Pier was clearly about

35

to spring to an alarming life in his mind.

The opening ceremony, after an incredible chapter of accidents and near disasters, took place on 30 June 1880. One of the speakers, charged with proposing the toast to the magistrates and town council of Oban, chose as his theme the open sewer that bordered the station frontage, then exhorted those members of his audience who came from Edinburgh to go home and tell their friends to *'try for themselves the salt water and pure air of Oban.'*

But neither access by rail or road, important though they are, determines Oban's place in the mainstream of Highland life. It is the sea that gives the town its unique quality. The seaways spread to Mull and Lismore, Staffa and Iona, Coll and sunny Tiree, reaching out as far as Barra and South Uist in the Outer Hebrides. The islands are Oban's distant suburbs, and the town – linked by the constant passage of the red-funnelled steamers – has the unmis-

takable ambience of the Gaelic West.

Mull of the mountains, moors, lochs, forested glens and towering sea-cliffs was cruelly shorn of its people in the last century, and the melancholy of that forced exodus has left lasting scars.

Outside the village of Dervaig, the ruins of a crofting township nestle in a green glade. Only the low walls of the croft houses are still standing. The irony of it is that the large, imposing house of the tacksman – that in a nineteenth-century crofting community must have represented the ultimate in secure stability – has also become an empty ruin. To compound the irony, the very emptiness of Mull in terms of an indigenous population is one of its potent attractions for those seeking a respite from an overcrowded urban environment.

There is much to delight the eye. Tobermory – seen from the stone jetty below Aros House on a still summer's evening – the main street

bounded by the harbour wall, yachts riding at anchor in the landlocked bay under the shield of the circling hills.

Or tiny Fionphort looking across the Sound of Iona to the grey abbey below the green sugarlump of Dun I.

The abbey, painstakingly restored by the Iona Community, is approached along the Street of the Dead, the ancient burial route of Scotland's kings. In Reilig Oran, 48 kings of Scotland, 4 of Ireland and 8 of Norway lie buried. For centuries a place of pilgrimage for the devout, it now caters for the modern pilgrim carrying not a staff, but camera and light meter.

The essence of the peace of Iona is to be found away from the over-trodden tourist trail in the farmlands above the sandy shores of the west coast. Here sky and sea and well-worked land weave a pastoral spell that is peculiarly Iona's own.

Opposite. The essence of the peace of Iona is to be found in the farmlands on the west coast of the island.

Above. Out from the heart of the hollow mountain to the Oban road through the Pass of Brander.

Below. The Cruachan reservoir high above Loch Awe.

37

Above. Clachan Bridge.
Opposite. Doom-laden Glencoe.

FORT WILLIAM AREA

In the time-scale of the geologist, the history of man on this planet would be measured in the blink of an eye. The rocks of Glencoe were shaped in the Tertiary period, scores of millions of years ago. They had weathered countless millenia before human life appeared on earth and the two-legged predator emerged from the steaming swamps and lifted covetous eyes to the hills.

The very aura of those hills turns the mind to thoughts of human tragedy rather than speculation on the awesome antiquity of their geological past. Glencoe is doom-laden; tragedy had to happen here. It is as if the ancient glaciers possessed a prescient spirit enabling them to forge a prophetic landscape, perpetuating in tortured rock a physical symbol of the vicious inhumanity of man to man.

The Great Herdsman of Etive, Buachaille Etive Mor, keeps watch over the desolate Moor of Rannoch and the Black Mount at the mouth of Glencoe. From the head of the glen, below a flat-topped rock – known in Gaelic as Innean a' Cheathaich, the Anvil of the Mist – the Coe plunges through a gorge under a high waterfall of the Allt Lairig Eilde. Precipitous rock faces surround the pass – a wild army of gaunt peaks, savaged by bleak ravines – heavy with brooding melancholy in rain and mist; towering in a fearsome, sombre majesty under snow.

At five o'clock on the morning of 13 February 1692, in the aftermath of a blizzard, the most infamous massacre in Scotland's gory history took place in this glen.

MacDonald men, women and children, who had billeted the soldier-assassins in their homes, were done to death by a company of Argyll's regiment under the command of Captain Robert Campbell of Glenlyon. It was murder

Above left. The crude sword thrust of the new bridge at
Ballachulish pierces the frontier of wild Lochaber.
Prior to the building of the bridge the road coiled
around the long arm of Loch Leven by way of the
isolated industrial village of Kinlochleven.

Above right. A singular memorial to an unknown navvy,
one of a Gaelic-speaking army who laboured at the turn
of the century to build the aluminium smelter at
Kinlochleven. A winter spent at the work camp in the
hills, toiling on the Blackwater dam, was enough to
impel many of them down the perilous Devil's Staircase
to the comforts of the Kingshouse Inn. For those
trapped in a blizzard, it was a costly drinking expedition.
Dying of cold and exposure, their nameless bodies were
often undiscovered until the winter snows had melted
in the spring.

under trust, universally regarded, even by seventeenth-century brigands weaned on the blood feud, as the foulest act of treachery known to man.

In Glencoe village, near the old Bridge of Coe, a tall Celtic cross commemorates the odious deed in words of moving simplicity; *In memory of MacIan, Chief of Glencoe, who fell with his people in the massacre of Glencoe.*

MacIan – 'the old fox' – has his lair on the little island of Eilean Munde in Loch Leven, opposite the foot of Glencoe, for centuries the burial place of the people of the glen.

The mere recollection of Glencoe made Charles Dickens shudder. *'The pass is an awful place,'* he wrote when recording impressions of his Highland tour in 1841. *'There are scores of glens high up, which form such haunts as you might imagine yourself wandering in in the very height and madness of a fever. They will live in my dreams for years – I was going to say as long as I live, and I seriously think so.'*

An even more illustrious – though less imaginative – traveller than Dickens was left with no such gloomy recollections after a visit to Glencoe. Queen Victoria thoroughly enjoyed a picnic in the glen in 1873. The royal party made their way from Clachaig Inn, then a stage for coaches between Fort William and Glasgow. Clachaig, at the western entrance to the glen, is on the old road from Ballachulish, a welcome sanctuary under the forbidding dark ridge of Aonach Dubh.

The royal picnic took place on the lofty eminence of The Study. By one of those curious corruptions to which language is prone,

The Study has become the meaningless English substitute for the beautifully poetic Gaelic, Anvil of the Mist. Overlooking the confluence of The Meeting of Three Waters, Innean a' Cheathaich, The Anvil of the Mist, commands a fine view of the Three Sisters of Glencoe, Beinn Fhada, Gearr Aonach and Aonach Dubh.

John Brown, who was always in close attendance at the Queen's Highland safaris, had little opportunity to admire the view. He was fully engaged in keeping an enterprising newspaper reporter at a respectful distance from his royal mistress.

Not all the old chief's clansmen died in the massacre of Glencoe. Some escaped in the snow through the high passes to the safety of Appin. Nowadays, the snow serves more peaceful pursuits, attracting climbers and

Above. Ardtoe in Ardnamurchan, the Point of the Great Ocean. Ardnamurchan is the most island-like of all the Highland peninsulas. Ardtoe, which houses an experiment in fish farming, looks out on Rhum and the towering Scuir of Eigg.

Above left. The strips of arable land of the crofters of Arisaig pattern the shore. With the dramatic silhouette of Eigg in view, Arisaig is an inviting springboard to the Small Isles.

43

Above. 'Concrete Bob's' viaduct soars high above the immense bowl at the head of Loch Shiel, enabling the rail traveller to look down on the tower monument to the 1745 Rising, and survey the entire reach of the loch.

Opposite. The wheeling, clamouring gulls of Mallaig, the greatest herring port in all Europe.

skiers to the freedom of the heights.

The north-easterly face of Meall a' Buridh has some of the finest ski-ing runs in Scotland, and the holding quality of the snow is such that these slopes invariably have a good cover long after others are bare. Access is easy. The old Glencoe road has been extended beyond Black Rock Cottage to a chalet, which is the starting point of a chair-lift up to 2100 feet. Above the chairlift, T-bar tows haul skiers up the remaining 1250 feet to the summit of the mountain.

After a day on the heights, skiers and climbers can foregather in the warmth and comfort of nearby Kingshouse Inn, haven of many a cold and hungry Glencoe traveller in the days when the inn signified safety as well as shelter.

The elongated village of Ballachulish lies at the foot of the glen on the shores of Loch Leven, an arm of Loch Linnhe. Its situation is picturesque enough to activate the most lethargic of cameramen, but in closeup the village is woefully down at heel. The detritus of the abandoned slate quarries – for two centuries the mainstay of employment in the district – scars the landscape; a sharp reminder of the need for restoration if the land is not to

be littered with industrial graveyards once the oil-boom is spent.

Much to the delight of the thousands of motorists who have fumed and fretted in long summer queues at the ferry, a bridge now spans the narrows to North Ballachulish. But there was something fitting about having to pause in order to gain access to Lochaber, and be ferried across water before breaching the frontier of 'the land of the mountain and the flood.' The bridge is a long overdue necessity, but the little ferry at Ballachulish had an off-beat charm all its own.

It was from 'Balichelie' on 12 February 1692, that Major Duncanson, an officer of scrupulous military exactitude, issued his final instructions to Campbell of Glenlyon; *'You are hereby ordered to fall upon the Rebells, the MacDonalds of Glencoe'*, the major wrote, with brutal candour, in a letter that is preserved in the National Library of Scotland in Edinburgh, *'and putt all to the sword under seventy, you are to have a speciall care that the old fox and his sones doe upon no account escape your hands, you are to secure all the avenues that no man escape. This you are to putt in executione at fyve of the clock precisely; and by that time or verie shortly after it, I'le strive*

to be att you with a stronger party: if I doe not come to you att fyve, you are not to tary for me, butt to fall on. This is by the King's speciall command and for the good and safety of the Country, that those miscreants be cutt off root and branch. See that this be putt in executione without feud or favour, else you may expect to be dealt with as one not true to King nor Government, nor a man fitt to cary Commissione in the King's service. Expecting you will not faill in the fulfilling hereof, as you love your selfe, I subscribe those with my hand att Balichelis feb; 12, 1692, for ther Ma(jes)ties service.'

The punctilious Major Duncanson – who was killed on active service in Spain at the siege of Valencia de Alcantara in 1705 – was an officer of the Fort William garrison, a strategically sited military bastion at the southern pivot of the Great Glen.

The old fort was obliterated by the relentless onward march of Victorian technology. All that remains today is the name, apart from the gateway to the fort which was dismantled and rebuilt to become the entrance to Craig Cemetery. Fort William, despite being tightly corseted by hill and loch, has contrived to expand between the steep slopes of Cow Hill and the waters of Loch Linnhe so that it is

45

Above left. The massif of hills ringing Glenfinnan were conquered by 'Concrete Bob' McAlpine and his army of anonymous navvies – Irishmen, Gaelic-speaking Highlanders and Lowland Scots. Miserably ill-equipped by modern standards, they fought through some of the toughest terrain in the country to extend the railway to Mallaig.

Above right. The lonely moor of Rannoch has a sombre majesty all its own.

Opposite. A tree-studded islet in the deep waters of Lochailort.

now the chief commercial and holiday centre of Lochaber.

The town's High Street is the unlikely springboard to country of so wild a magnificence that even a Petticoat Lane huckster would be lost for words at the sight of it. There is the mighty Mamore range, an ocean of rock rising in crested waves under the massive flank of Ben Nevis, and the lochs and glens of Eil, Arkaig and Garry, magical in the misty, milky, early-morning Lochaber light, creating the illusion of a new-born world awaiting the coming of a wide-eyed Adam. And if the perverse old Ben has brought the rainclouds down upon his head, there is always the Bingo Hall

in Fort William's High Street, or – more profitably – the West Highland Museum with its three floors of exhibits.

The town itself is lumbered with a crippling legacy from its Victorian burghers. In their anxiety to attract the railway to Fort William, they were blind to the consequences of allowing the line to follow the shore of Loch Linnhe to the pier at the south end of the town; a miscalculation in the aesthetics of town-planning equivalent to converting the canals of Venice into an inner ring-road system. Access to the shore is effectively blocked, and succeeding generations have been denied the pleasure of a lochside esplanade fronting Loch

Linnhe. On the other hand, Fort William railwaymen with an eye for scenic beauty have enjoyed the benefit of a station and signal box built on the shores of the loch.

In 1889, when the railway engineers appeared on the scene, they discovered that the Fort William line would have to pass through the old, disused fort. The walls were unbreached, although the barrack blocks had been converted into dwelling houses and the fosse transformed into a cabbage patch. As the site was scheduled to become an engine shed, the engineers set about demolishing the ancient fortifications, an operation not without its surprises. Cannon balls were dug out

47

Above. The Mallaig line noses under the massive
shoulder of Ben Nevis and heads west by Loch Eil.
The pulp and paper mill on the shores of the loch is a
mere pimple when set against the bulk of the mighty Ben.

Opposite. A man-made mountain of wood chips rising to
meet the insatiable appetite of the pulp mill.

of the old walls, coins were unearthed and a
male skeleton was found in the ramparts.
Greater hazards awaited the construction
gangs as they struggled across the wastes of
Rannoch Moor, but on 11 August 1894 – as a
precursor to the then all-important 'Glorious
Twelfth' – the West Highland line from
Glasgow to Fort William was ceremonially
opened amidst scenes of great rejoicing.

But it is the Mallaig extension – started on
21 January 1897, when Lady Margaret Cameron of Lochiel cut the first sod in a field at
Corpach – that seizes the imagination, even to
this day. Built on the cheap in a brief four
years, and involving the greatest concentration
of mass concrete construction – at that time a
novel, untried medium – that the nineteenth-
century world had ever seen, the line is a
prodigious feat of engineering.

The hirsute Victorians, despite their be-
whiskered image, were no worshippers of
doddering age. 'Concrete Bob' McAlpine
appointed his son Robert, aged 28, to take

full charge of construction, assisted by his younger son Malcolm who was two years short of his 21st birthday. It was young Malcolm who devised a system of water turbines to power the rock drills for the miles of cuttings and tunnels needed on the Mallaig line.

The prosaically named Mallaig extension is a living monument to the incredible toil of thousands of anonymous navvies – Irishmen, Gaelic-speaking Highlanders and Lowland Scots – and the indomitable engineering genius of 'Concrete Bob' McAlpine.

Starting from the toy station on the banks of Loch Linnhe, the line passes close to the ruins of Inverlochy Castle and a more recent landmark the pulp and paper mill complex, then noses impudently under the flank of the mighty Ben, and heads west by Loch Eil to the islands.

On into the mountains and through the narrow pass to the great bowl at the head of Loch Shiel, ringed by a massif of hills, and bridged by the curving Glenfinnan viaduct –

more than 100 feet high, an engineering work of art, the 21 slender, pillared arches a revolutionary poem in poured concrete – the whole reach of the long loch open to view, crowned by the tower monument to the ill-fated 1745 Rising.

A first sight of the sea at Loch nan Uamh; Arisaig, with the Small Isles – Canna, Rhum, Eigg and Muck – swimming on the horizon; Morar of the delectable sands; and then, when it seems that only anti-climax can follow, the wheeling, clamouring gulls heralding the advent of Mallaig, greatest herring port in all Europe.

Miserably ill-equipped by modern standards, 'Concrete Bob' and his army of navvies fought their way through some of the toughest territory in the country to reach Mallaig. Such a feat should have adequate public recognition if justice is to be done to his memory. Before the centenary of the line is celebrated, it should be ceremonially re-named 'The "Concrete Bob" Special.'

SPEY VALLEY

Opposite. The high Cairngorms. Above. The Feshie river.

Spring, summer, autumn and winter, every accent known to the British Isles, plus a fair sprinkling from Europe, the Commonwealth and North America, can be heard in the Spey Valley.

The old concept of a brief summer season is dead, its obsequies sounding in the merry ring of cash registers the whole year through. Enthusiasts of the new regime claim that there has been an infectious infusion of fresh life, energy and gaiety, transforming standards. They point to the fact that even the chill Victorian mausoleums, which once held gloomy sway masquerading as hotels, have followed the trend-setters in providing a milieu fit for après-ski addicts eager for all the creature comforts when they descend from the snow slopes.

Such affirmations do not meet with universal acclaim. Ecologists and ornithologists deplore the bulldozing of slopes, where the greenshank once nested, to provide a freeway for skiers. They bemoan a too-easy access to the high tops of the Cairngorms, and the long-term effect of a mass influx on the wilderness heights.

One point is beyond dispute; the natural assets of Speyside are legion. Shielded by the vast massif of the Cairngorms with their semi-permanent snowfields, beguilingly remote corries, high tundras, alpine flora, and wonderfully varied wildlife, the long Valley of the Spey is the ideal location for active recreation in surroundings of great natural beauty.

This is an area larger than Greater London and the County of Kent combined. It contains within its boundaries the 60,000-acre Cairngorm Nature Reserve, home of the ptarmigan, dotterel, golden eagle, mountain hare, red deer, reindeer, and the tiny, indomitable snow bunting, which nests in the ridges and corries of the arctic high tops.

There are rivers and lochs world renowned for their salmon and trout fishing; exhilarating snow slopes to tempt the skier, with expert coaching on safe nursery slopes available for young – and old – beginners; camping sites beyond compare in Glenmore Forest Park, which extends along the shores of Loch Morlich; a multitude of glens and wooded straths, the preserve of walkers and pony-trekkers, where the only sound is the purl of a hill stream over its rocky bed, and the world of motorways, transistors and high-rise flats seems to belong to another planet. Add a scatter of holiday villages – Aviemore, Boat of Garten, Carrbridge, Grantown-on-Spey, Kincraig, Kingussie, Nethybridge, Newtonmore – which grew up in times less frenetic than our own, and the potent attraction of Speyside is manifest.

Grouped around the 70-acre site fronting the Craigellachie Nature Trail, the Aviemore Centre could be said to have followed a trail blazed by the late Lord Fraser of Allander. Lord Fraser headed a consortium of wealthy businessmen whose aim was the creation of a totally self-contained holiday village. It was the most ambitious project of its kind ever undertaken in this country, hailed by the

economists – with their customary felicity of phrase – as a major investment in the leisure industry. Since its opening in December 1966, it has certainly been a major attraction for holidaymakers.

The Aviemore Centre consists of a complex of hotels and a motel with 'Swiss-style' chalets; the superbly equipped Speyside Theatre seating 720; exhibition halls; conference and banqueting suites; Britain's second largest indoor ice-skating and curling rink; a 25-metre indoor, heated swimming pool; a wide range of restaurants, grill rooms and snack bars; children's playrooms, with trained attendants on hand to check incipient mayhem among the small-fry; and a sprinkling of shops stocked with the craft products of the Highlands. No section of the holiday market has been overlooked. For those who prefer to travel with their own home on wheels, there is a caravan park near the Fishing Centre at Loch Puladdern. All the facilities within the Centre are open to non-residents.

The mediocrity of the architecture of the Aviemore Centre is sadly at odds with the majestic scale of the landscape. This assortment of geometric concrete blocks constitutes an offence against nature in the shape of the Monadhliath mountains and the mighty Cairngorms. The Scandinavian-style Rank complex at Coylumbridge merges much more happily with its surroundings.

Not surprisingly, Aviemore has become synonomous with winter sports. The access road in Coire Cas ends at the car-park, a

Opposite. A Cairngorm deer stalk in spacious Edwardian days.

Above. A Cairngorm deer stalk in the straitened 1970s.

Overleaf. The wilderness beauty of the high tops.

Known to anglers the world over, the River Spey sweeps majestically through the valley that bears its name.

startling 2000 feet above sea-level, and only a short walk from the bottom terminal of the chairlift. With five T-bar tows in Coire Cas, 4500 skiers an hour can be whisked up to the high slopes.

The middle station of the chairlift links up with the White Lady Shieling, notable for the incongruous call-box plonked down outside the entrance, looking as if it has newly descended from the sky. Hot drinks and snacks are dispensed at the White Lady, and a licensed restaurant on the upper floor deals with the more substantial needs of those made suddenly ravenous by the invigorating mountain air. Perched beside the top terminal is the Ptarmigan Observation Restaurant, an impertinent pimple on the majestic brow of Cairngorm, but at 3650 feet indisputably the highest restaurant in Great Britain.

The broad flank of the mountain imposes

its own vast scale. Looking down on the crowded slopes, the human figures are dramatically reduced in size, for all the world like the tiny, miniaturized creatures Lowry painted against industrial backgrounds.

The osprey hide near Loch Garten has little in common with the unisex gear and raffish dark glasses of the hotching ski slopes. Silence and stillness reap a rich reward here, enabling the watcher to study at close quarters those aloof aristocrats of the air, the great fish-eating hawks.

The return of the osprey to nest successfully on a Scots fir in Strathspey in the 1950s, after a barren gap of more than half a century, represents a triumph for those dedicated to the preservation of bird-life.

Osprey feathers were once in great demand to adorn the hats of fashionable ladies. Avid collectors salivated at the thought of acquiring osprey eggs, which seemed to hone their acquisitive instincts to a razor sharpness. Desmond Nethersole-Thompson, who watched the first of the returning ospreys through a telescope from the window of his house, has described the lure of a nest of osprey eggs; *'. . . big eggs, two or three of them, of creamy-ground colour, almost completely covered with great blood-red blotches and violet under-markings.'* The inoffensive fish-eating hawk was indiscriminately slaughtered for its plumage, and had its eggs seized for the collector. By the beginning of this century, the osprey had been liquidated as a nesting species in Scotland, although the breed continued to nest successfully in Sweden and Finland.

It was in the early 1950s that a handful of excited Scottish ornithologists began to report to their colleagues on the return of the osprey. It is thought that a pair from Scandinavia,

Above left. The mountain imposes its own vast scale.
Looking down from the crowded ski slopes, human
figures are dramatically reduced in size, like the tiny
stick figures L. S. Lowry painted against an industrial
background.

Above right. Skiers on Coire Cas.

Above. Grouped around a 70-acre site fronting the
Craigellachie Nature Trail, the Aviemore Centre caters
for all sections of the holiday market. It was hailed by
the economists – with their customary felicity of phrase –
as a major investment in the leisure industry.

passing over Strathspey on their northward migration in spring and seeing a territory bearing a striking resemblance to their homeland, took the happy decision to nest here. They built an eyrie, but the nest was robbed, doubtless to become an expensive addition to some wealthy collector's private hoard.

To combat the egg thieves, the Royal Society for the Protection of Birds organized 'Operation Osprey.' The first year, despite a careful watch, the eggs vanished on the exceptionally dark and misty night of 3 June. Since that setback, the defences have been constantly strengthened, and a day and night, round the clock watch is mounted the moment the ospreys arrive. The only unsuccessful years were 1963 and 1966, when gales destroyed the nest and eggs and, more recently, when a human predator evaded the defences, although he was subsequently charged and had to suffer the ignominy of public exposure.

The eyrie is on the crown of an old Scots fir growing on a small dry knoll in typical greenshank country. Many observers have commented on the curious way in which ospreys obtain nest-building material, flying to an old pine tree, hovering over a dead branch and then breaking a stick off without

alighting. On a still day, the sharp crack as the stick snaps can be heard clearly.

Visitors to the osprey hide have rare delights in store for them. The osprey is in supreme command of its element, and to see it in lazy, gliding flight is to witness a poetic arabesque in the air. The lucky ones may see the cock bird hovering over the eyrie with a fresh-caught trout in his talons, or observe the young doing vigorous wing exercises prior to becoming airborne for the first time. It is doubtful if any immigrant has ever been so cherished, or afforded so much pleasure to so many.

Grantown-on-Spey, the capital of Strathspey, can claim the distinction of being one of Scotland's oldest 'new towns.' Cromdale was the chief centre of population in the reign of James VI, and had its position confirmed by royal edict, being elevated by the monarch to burgh status. But local government in Strathspey was concentrated in the person of Sir Ludovic Grant of Grant, who had rather more grandiose schemes than his king, and – unlike his royal master – the means on the ground to execute them. Finding Cromdale displeasing, Sir Ludovic decided to go back to the drawing board and create an entirely new town.

The response to his initial advertisement

59

was less than enthusiastic, but the first house was completed in 1766, marking the birth of Grantown. Present inhabitants must bless the fact that, as well as a desire to perpetuate his own name, Sir Ludovic possessed a discerning eye for a good site. After his death, the work was carried on by his son, Sir James Grant. He built roads, bridges and the courthouse, setting the style and shape of a town worthy of its location.

On 4 September 1860, Queen Victoria – travelling incognito, with the ubiquitous Brown one of the party – spent a night in the Grant Arms Hotel after a strenuous pony-trekking expedition from Balmoral, by way of Glen Feshie. The royal party crossed the Spey by ferry near Loch Insh. *'It was,'* the Queen recorded in her journal, *'a very rude affair, like a boat or coble, but we could only stand on it, and it was moved at one end by two long oars, plied by the ferryman and Brown, and at the other end by a long sort of beam.'* Once across the river, the Queen and Prince Albert – whose comments, alas, were not recorded – transferred to a *'shabby vehicle, a kind of barouche, drawn by a pair of small and rather miserable horses,'* for the three hours drive to Grantown.

Dinner at the Grant Arms *'was very fair, and all very clean – soup, "hodge-podge", mutton-broth with vegetables, which I did not much relish, fowl with white sauce, good roast lamb, very good potatoes, besides one or two other dishes which I did not taste, ending with a good dish of cranberries.'*

The indefatigable royal sightseer had her party out in the morning for a quick sortie by coach to Castle Grant, the seat of Lord Seafield. The Queen was not impressed. *'A very plain-looking house,'* she confided to her journal, *'like a factory, about two miles from the town,'* adding caustically, *'We did not get out.'* One can only hope that poor Lord Seafield wasn't lurking behind the net curtains waiting to welcome his sovereign.

North east of Grantown, the remains of a ruined castle can be seen on an island in Lochindorb. Ruined castles abound in the Highlands, scenically sited on islets in lonely lochs, but the castle of Lochindorb has associations as grim as any Dracula-haunted keep in Transylvania. The castle was the lair of the Wolf of Badenoch, a fourteenth-century thug of horrific reputation whose brief life seems to have been devoted to murder and rapine. Six centuries later, the fearsome Wolf of Badenoch has had his historic come-uppance, subjected to the ultimate indignity by having a bar in the Aviemore Centre named after him.

Rothiemurchus, the Great Plain of the Pines, is the haunt of some of the most fascinating of our native birds. The patient watcher will see a small grey bird with a curious little crest, white cheeks and a black bib. This is the famous crested tit, a relic of the post-glacial pine forests. Another relict bird to be seen is the Scottish parrot crossbill; the cock arrayed in scarlet, the hen green with a bright yellow rump-patch. This is the home of Scotland's biggest game bird, the capercaillie, whose mating rampage can shatter the quiet of a spring dawn. Then there is the spectacle of the blackcock, parading the forest clearings displaying their lyre-shaped tails as they engage in their strange ritual dances.

The Rothiemurchus forest has been decimated by the depredations brought about by the desperate need for timber during two world wars. But at the beginning of the last century, the great firs of the forest massed

The gaunt ruins of Ruthven Barracks; a sombre reminder of the days when the rebellious Highlands were under the jackboot of the Hanoverian military.

across the plain between the River Spey and the mountains. The Spey and its host of tributaries were the open arteries of the forest, and the dams and sluice gates in the hill-lochs controlled the run of water.

The Spey 'floaters' – men who had followed the calling for generations and knew every rock and shoal and current in the river – floated the felled timber down the long course of the river to the sea.

The floaters were based in a windowless bothy at the mouth of the River Druie. Conditions were far from luxurious. There was a fire on a stone hearth in the middle of the floor; a hole in the centre of the thatched roof prevented asphyxiation and the earthen floor was spread with heather which served as a communal bed. After a day's work in the river preparing their rafts, the floaters, wrapped in their sodden plaids, lay down for the night each man with his feet to the fire; a circle of bodies enveloped in a fug of steam and peat reek.

The floaters drilled two deep holes in each end of the logs by auger, and hammered eyeletted iron plugs into the holes. Twisted wattles were passed through the eyes of the plugs binding the logs together to form a crude raft. Cut deal made a rough decking, and on these primitive rafts the floaters ferried the Rothiemurchus logs down the length of the Spey to the timber yard near Fochabers, where they were sorted and stacked for sale. All that remains of those brave days are the stones of the dams at the south end of Loch Morlich and the north end of Loch Eunach.

It is the Spey, rising in the Monadhliath mountains and gathering strength as it sweeps majestically through the valley it has made its own, that mirrors the history of the land.

INVERNESS AND LOCH NESS

Opposite. Loch Affric. Above. The River Ness.

Top. Britain's first industrial hydro-electric power station and aluminium smelter was built at Foyers, on the shores of Loch Ness, in 1894. Conceived by the great Victorian innovator, Lord Kelvin, an infant industry mushroomed from this unlikely base into a world-wide colossus.

Bottom. After Culloden, ruined Fort George – the ancient Castle of Inverness – was abandoned, and a new Fort George was constructed at Ardersier; a grandiose replacement costing £160,000. Equally attractive to the movie buff and the military historian, this incredible Hollywood confection – tailor-made for a costume epic on the grand scale – is the home of the Regimental Museum of the Seaforth Highlanders and the Queen's Own Cameron Highlanders.

Inverness is one of the oldest inhabited localities in Scotland. Centuries before the first Christian missionary brought word of the new religion, men hunted and fished here. They founded permanent settlements, fortified hills, constructed intricate burial cairns and raised memorials to their unknown gods.

Their choice of locality was determined by the hard facts of geography; the one constant in the town's long history. Poised at the eastern entrance to the Great Glen of Scotland – the magnificently scenic rift of Glean mor-nan Albyn – Inverness is the strategic hub of the region.

To the north, south and west, the town is ringed by mountains. Its open eastern flank is protected by the Firth of Inverness, a moat formed by the long, curving beak of the Fort George peninsula pecking at Chanonry Point on the Black Isle shore. The massive bulk of Ben Wyvis – as reassuringly familiar a local landmark to Invernessians as Big Ben is to Londoners – rears high in the north west, with the peaks of Strathglass and Wester Ross lifting on the skyline. The Valley of the Ness cleaves a passage through the hills to the south west, with the rounded top of Mealfuarvonie the dominant watch-keep over Loch Ness. On the south side, the massed ranks of the Monadhliadh, the Grey Mountains, complete the encirclement.

The first written word of Inverness is to be found in Adamnan's *'Life of Saint Columba.'* In the sixth century AD the wandering Columba is reputed to have stood before the great wooden gates of the fortress of King Brude beside the Ness. Adamnan is vague on the exact location of the stronghold of the Pictish king, but only a pedant would quibble at equating *'beside the Ness'* with the site of the present town, cleft by the same river.

What is beyond dispute is that the ancient Castle of Inverness stood on the 'Crown' to the east of the present Castlehill. After the death of Duncan – immortalized in Shakespeare's *'MacBeth'* – the castle met an equally violent end, being burned to the ground. All that remains today is the name of the site, Auld Castlehill, its past notoriety sedately buried beneath the solid masonry of Victorian villas.

The first stone-built keep on the present Castlehill – a commanding eminence above the River Ness – came into being during the reign of King David I, who created Inverness a royal burgh in the twelfth century. In the course of time, the town gradually grew under the protective shade of Castlehill, where a royal fortress crowned the summit for six centuries.

The early kings of Scotland were frequent visitors, although a royal progress north rarely heralded a peaceful visitation. They were usually in response to the activities of the unruly clans, who regarded Inverness as the symbol of an alien law and order.

In the spring of 1427, James I convened a parliament in Inverness and took up residence in the castle. The naively unsuspecting Highland chiefs accepted the royal invitation to attend, and 40 of them were promptly imprisoned. Two minor chiefs were executed, but this drastic deterrent did not quell the King's turbulent subjects. After a year in captivity, Alexander, Lord of the Isles, celebrated his release by pillaging and burning the town.

In November 1651, the town was occupied by a Commonwealth force. The following year, work began on a mighty pentagonal-shaped citadel to hold a garrison of 1000 men and 600 horse. It was designed by Major-General Deane, who obtained most of his stone from the plundered cathedral at Fortrose.

The west side of the citadel fronted the River Ness, and the other four sides were surrounded by a wide moat fed from the river at full tide. The main entrance was on the north side, approached by a drawbridge of heavy oak timbers.

A formidable, square, stone building stood in the centre of the citadel. The ground floor contained the granary, whilst the top floor – with a truly Cromwellian sense of the fitness of things – was reserved for the garrison's church.

The Inverness Pentagon cost £80,000, an enormous sum in seventeenth-century terms. But like so many military extravaganzas it was destined for a swift and inglorious end. Following the restoration of Charles II, the citadel was demolished in 1661 and served as a quarry for much of the new building in the town. All that is left today of Cromwell's Pentagon is the clock tower, forlornly marking time on Shell's oil storage tanks.

On 28 September 1664, the old wooden bridge across the Ness gave up the ghost and collapsed. The town was without a bridge across the river for 21 years, which must constitute something of a record in local inertia. Eventually £1300 was raised by voluntary subscriptions throughout the kingdom, and a new bridge of seven arches – the first stone bridge in the Highlands – was built. The new bridge incorporated the novel feature of a prison cell in one of the arches, which later served an even more bizarre purpose – to house 'dangerous lunatics.'

But a sense of civic pride was slowly awakening. In 1688, Provost Dunbar sponsored the building of an alms house in Church Street for the poor of the town. The old building still presents a brave face to the world; one infinitely more pleasing than the latest additions to the town centre. Its near neighbour, Abertarff House – present home of *An Comunn Gaidhealach*, the Gaelic language protection society – contains the last remaining example of the old turnpike stair. The stones for both buildings were taken from the ruins of Cromwell's citadel; poetic justice for the sacking of Fortrose Cathedral.

In 1715 – with the connivance of the magistrates – the Jacobites captured the castle and proclaimed the Old Pretender as king. The revolt was short-lived. The castle was re-captured, and subsequently rebuilt by General Wade. The General – a stout believer in the old military maxim that superiors exist to be flattered – renamed the castle Fort George, in honour of his Hanoverian king.

Although the magistrates took care not to back a second Stuart loser, the town suffered severely in the aftermath of the 1745 Rising. Initially, the forces of Prince Charles occupied Inverness, the garrison surrendering ignominiously after a two-day siege. The castle was then blown up on the orders of the Prince by his French engineer.

16 April 1746 brought a harsher occupation than any experienced in the past. With the rout of the retreating remnants of the Jacobite army at Culloden – the last battle to be fought on British soil – the victorious soldiers of Augustus, Duke of Cumberland, exacted a savage revenge. Homes were ransacked, the Episcopal chapel destroyed, the parish church and the Gaelic church turned into prisons, the grammar school converted into the army's commissary, and the town hall commandeered as army headquarters. A number of prisoners were summarily shot in the parish churchyard and their bodies thrown into a common grave.

The mailed fist of Butcher Cumberland clamped down on the town, although it must be recorded that the oppressor was responsible for a much needed innovation. At that time, garbage of all kinds was tossed into the street in the sanguine expectation that it would be washed away by rain. According to the town's records, it was Cumberland who ordered the streets to be swept at the public expense. It is a curious footnote to the tragedy of Culloden that the dreaded Duke, so insensitive to human suffering, should have been the fastidious founder of the town's cleansing department.

Ruined Fort George – the ancient Castle of Inverness – was abandoned, and a new Fort George constructed at Ardersier; a grandiose replacement costing £160,000. But as the military occupation eased, civil building began to get under way again. In 1791, a new academy was built by public subscription, and a new town steeple and tolbooth replaced the old prison.

The nineteenth century ushered in an era of rapid expansion, notable for the building of the Caledonian Canal, an immense engineering project taking two decades to complete, master-minded by the great Thomas Telford. Outside the offices of the Caledonian Canal

Opposite. Loch Ness, unscathed by tawdry gimmickry,
despite its international tourist billing as the home of the
fabled 'monster'.

Above. A lazy spiral of smoke drifts above
Drumnadrochit, the half-way house to Fort Augustus.

Above. Master-minded by the indomitable Thomas Telford, the Caledonian Canal took two decades to complete. Linking Loch Ness, Loch Oich and Loch Lochy, it cleaves through the spectacular rift of Glean mor-nan Albyn to Fort William and the western sea. The canal is an enduring monument to Telford's tenacity and engineering genius. Increasingly used by leisure craft, this unique waterway provides the means for the ideal holiday afloat.

Opposite. Abertarff House – home of An Comunn Gaidhealach, the Gaelic language protection society – contains the last remaining example in Inverness of the old turnpike stair, once the coveted status symbol of every wealthy burgher.

Company, a marble slab carries Poet Laureate Robert Southey's fulsome tribute to his friend Telford;

'Where these capacious basins by the laws
Of the subjacent element, receive
The Ship, descending or upraised, eight
  times,
From stage to stage with unfelt agency
Translated, fitliest may the marble here
Record the Architect's immortal Name.
TELFORD it was by whose presiding mind
The whole great work was planned and
  perfected.'

Few friendships could have survived such an execrable effusion, but the old Scots engineer was a man of stoic character.

A new courthouse was erected on Castlehill on the site of the ancient Castle of Inverness. It was described by a contemporary chronicler as a handsome castellated building; a bland euphemism for a touch of the old Victorian gothic-baronials. The Highland Railway Company opened its first line – Inverness to Nairn – in 1855, and forged ahead with more ambitious projects linking the far north to the great cities of the south.

The revolution in transport brought an increasing number of visitors to Inverness, and sparked off a boom in hotel building. Advertising-men competed in extravagant name-dropping. The Highland Railway Company's new Station Hotel in Inverness proudly proclaimed that it was, *'Patronised by their Royal Highnesses the Prince and Princess of Wales, the Duke of Cambridge, Prince and Princess Christian, and other Members of the Royal Family, and by most of the Nobility of Europe.'* Pianos were at the disposal of the occupants in every private sitting-room at no extra charge, but a cold bath added a shilling to the bill.

The old town, huddled under the castle on the hill, has gone. Merchants no longer gather every morning at the Mercat Cross, meeting point of the four main streets. Gone are the red sandstone houses with stepped gables and turnpike stairs – the upper galleries hanging so low over the narrow streets that the dragoons of Cumberland's Guard had to crouch over the manes of their horses as they rode by. But Inverness has managed to retain its twelfth-century designation, *capitalis per totum regnum*, one of the chief places in the Kingdom.

One of its chief attractions is on the doorstep of the town, that most famous of all lochs – Loch Ness. Despite its international billing as the home of the fabled 'monster', the loch remains miraculously unscathed by tawdry gimmickry. A favourite spot for sightings of the beastie is Castle Urquhart – nobly sited overlooking the bay at the foot of Glen Urquhart – for centuries a stronghold of the powerful Seafield Grants.

Robert Burns visited the loch on his Highland tour, and left behind the obligatory verse on a famous beauty spot. The national bard must have been the victim of Highland hospitality, for his turgid offering, *'Written With A Pencil, Standing By The Fall Of Fyers, Near Loch-Ness'*, reeks of a bad hangover.

It was at Foyers that the great Victorian innovator, Lord Kelvin, built Britain's first industrial hydro-electric power station and aluminium smelter in 1894. From this unlikely Highland source an infant industry has mushroomed into a world-wide colossus.

Victorian tourists travelling through the Caledonian Canal had a surprise in store for them at Fort Augustus. There was always the chance of an encounter with Roualeyn George Gordon Cumming, an aristocratic eccentric,

whose contribution to the gaiety of Highland life has never been fully recognized. Followed by his manservant and a long-bearded goat, he would invite passengers to inspect his famous museum collection, at a 'bob a nob', while their boat negotiated the canal locks.

Gordon Cumming was an attraction as unusual as his collection of skins and heads. He sported a kilt and plaid of Gordon tartan with topboots, frilled shirt and masses of jewels, a brass helmet on his head and silver fish-hooks in his ears. An enthusiastic nudist, he discarded his kilt on hot days.

Five of the loveliest glens in the Highlands – Glen Cannich, Glen Strathfarrar, Glen Affric, Glen Moriston and Glen Shiel – lie within easy reach of Inverness. But it would be an injustice to the town to regard it merely as a convenient springboard to the hills, glens and lochs of its hinterland.

Inverness is the meeting place of the vast Highland region; its streets, shops, restaurants, cafés and hotels a familiar sight to the Gaelic-speaking crofter from the Outer Hebrides, the sheep farmer from a lonely mainland strath, the rural housewife out on a shopping spree. It has an ambience compounded of all these elements.

As for the stranger, few fail to climb Castle-hill and gaze down on the Ness curving through the many-spired town in a broad sweep to the sea. And few fail to return.

WESTER ROSS

Opposite. Castle Urquhart. Above. Stac Polly.

Even the most dedicated economist – one who was weaned on tables of statistics, cut his teeth on multi-coloured graphs, and sublimated his adolescent libido by a total immersion in the cold complexities of the Gross National Product – would be hard-pushed to keep his mind on the economic facts of life in Wester Ross. The landscape is of so stark a grandeur that it cuts human pretensions down to size. Man – even expert man, encased in a little brief authority – is compelled to stop and stare and reflect. Senses that have atrophied under an urban carapace slowly stir to life. The rain has a different feel; the elusive sun, when he deigns to appear, a fiercer glare; the wind, soughing through the high corries, a pre-hensile touch. There is no cosy domesticity about this land. The elements command.

Ranging north west of the Great Glen, sparsely populated Wester Ross harbours re-doubts as wild and remote as any in the length and breadth of the Highlands. With its moun-tainous, deeply indented seaboard forming a rough-hewn rampart against the stormy waters of the North Minch, it is a natural refuge for wildlife. The eagle, ptarmigan and raven share the lonely heights with herds of red deer and the lordly wild cat.

Of all the roads to the incomparable west, there is none better than the route from Inver-ness by way of Invermoriston. The road skirts Loch Cluanie and plunges down through mountain-hemmed Glen Shiel before bursting out on the open reach of Loch Duich into Kintail.

The Five Sisters assert their ascendancy over Kintail, every sharply etched line of these mountain peaks exuding a hard, masculine power strangely at variance with their feminine gender; Highland Amazons, conscious of their supremacy. Against such a backdrop, the castle of Eilean Donan has a toy-like quality not normally associated with fortresses.

The castle stands on a tiny islet close to the meeting place of the waters of Loch Duich, Loch Alsh and Loch Long. Linked to the mainland shore by a triple-arched bridge and causeway over a strip of tidal water, this fairy-tale confection in a fabulous setting has been a godsend to the purveyors of shortbread. Romantic Eilean Donan has been pressed into service as the beguiling centrepiece on count-less thousands of tartan-wreathed tins.

The castle is a twentieth-century recon-struction of an ancient medieval fortress. As the rebuilding cost a quarter of a million

pounds, it must rate as one of the most expensive castles in Scotland.

In 1912, Eilean Donan Castle – no more than a picturesque ruin – was acquired by Lieutenant-Colonel John MacRae-Gilstrap, whose forbears had once been Constables of Eilean Donan. The Colonel's American wife shared his missionary zeal for restoration and the costly enterprise was embarked upon. Interrupted by the First World War, the work took twenty years to complete, and the restored castle is now open to the public.

The great banqueting hall houses a collection of Jacobite trophies and relics, for the castle played a major role in those rebellious days, at one time being garrisoned by the Spanish allies of the Old Pretender. The stone canopy above the huge fireplace is decorated with the MacRae coat of arms, flanked by the banners of the Black Watch; a curious irony, as the regiment was employed by the Hanoverian Government to extirpate dissident Jacobites in the Highlands.

The old fortress of Eilean Donan, which had survived an assault by the war-galleys of Donald Grumach of Sleat in 1539, finally met a bizarre end almost 200 years later. After the failure of the Jacobite rebellion in 1715, James

Opposite left. Romantic Eilean Donan Castle, rock-fast on a tiny islet close to the meeting place of the waters of Loch Duich, Loch Alsh and Loch Long. The castle is a twentieth-century reconstruction of the ancient medieval fortress which was destroyed in 1719.

Top. George Keith, the youthful Earl Marischal of Scotland, a military prodigy who later gained glory as a distinguished mercenary in the service of Frederick the Great of Prussia.

Bottom. The worldly Cardinal Alberoni, a principal supporter of the abortive Jacobite invasion of 1719.

Above. Loch Maree – with its lochside forests and pine-clad islands – fringes the Beinn Eighe National Nature Reserve.

Opposite. Bealach na Bo – The Pass of the Cattle – the precipitous mountain road to the village of Applecross on the far west of the peninsula.

Francis Edward Stuart, the luckless *Chevalier de Saint Georges* and pretender to the British throne, fled to his 'court' at Bar-le-Duc in Lorraine. The Old Pretender had not abandoned all hope of regaining the British crown, and he still had powerful supporters in Europe. Charles XII of Sweden was prepared to provide invasion troops, and the militant Cardinal Alberoni, chief minister of Phillip of Spain, was willing to dip into the Spanish Treasury to aid the impoverished Jacobites.

By 1719, invasion plans had matured, the main impetus coming from Spain. Cardinal Alberoni organized the major invasion force under the command of the Duke of Ormonde,

James Stuart's shadow Prime Minister, for a landing in the West of England. George Keith, Earl Marischal of Scotland was provided with two frigates and a few companies of Spanish troops. The youthful Earl Marischal was to effect a diversionary landing in the West Highlands, and raise the sympathetic clans.

But ill-fortune and ineptitude – constant companions of the Jacobites – soon made their presence felt. The inconsiderate Charles XII got himself killed in battle, thereby removing Swedish participation at a stroke. Inept to the bitter end, James Stuart – after a farcical undercover cloak-and-dagger flit from Rome – arrived in Spain too late to join the main invasion fleet which had already sailed from Cadiz. For one so prone to sea-sickness, the Old Pretender's luck was in. The fleet fell foul of a tremendous storm in the Bay of Biscay, and the crippled survivors were forced to limp back to their home ports.

Meantime, Keith's mini-fleet had made a landfall on the Island of Lewis in the Outer Hebrides at the end of March. In true Jacobite fashion, days were wasted in determining who was to command the expedition on land and the strategy to be employed. The two frigates eventually sailed into the sheltered waters of Loch Alsh on 14 April, and dropped anchor at the clan MacKenzie stronghold of Castle Eilean Donan.

Safely ensconced in the fortress, they occupied their time in more pointless squabbling. The only decisive action was taken by young Keith. When news reached him of the failure of the Duke of Ormonde's fleet to cross the Bay of Biscay, he ordered the two frigates to put to sea. Had he not acted swiftly, the ships would have been trapped by the British navy.

Full details of the invasion plans had been known to the British Government from the outset of the ill-starred expedition, and a naval squadron of five ships was closing in on the stranded invaders. The *Assistance* and *Dartmouth* anchored in Loch Kishorn to the north. Captain Boyle, commander of the squadron, sailed up Loch Alsh with the *Flamborough, Enterprise* and *Worcester* to storm Eilean Donan. The tiny garrison of 45 Spaniards surrendered after a token resistance, and the ancient fortress was blown up.

The scene was now set for the Battle of Glenshiel, although the Jacobites had to wait until 5 June before the ultra-cautious General

A strong pulse of energetic life is beating in lonely Loch Kishorn. Close to Kishorn Island where Captain Boyle's anti-Jacobite naval squadron lay at anchor in the summer of 1719, a giant concrete oil-production platform is under construction.

Wightman marched out of Inverness with his force of a thousand men. The Highlanders – whose motley ranks included followers of Rob Roy Macgregor, Scotland's most famous outlaw and a few hundred wretched Spaniards – held positions close to the old Bridge of Shiel, where the ground rises steeply to the hills. On the morning of 10 June 1719, Lord George Murray reported that General Wightman had struck his camp at Loch Cluanie and was marching towards Glenshiel. It was the luckless Old Pretender's birthday, the worst omen of all for the Jacobites.

The two armies came within sight of each other at two o'clock in the afternoon. Fighting began between five and six o'clock. The Battle of Glenshiel was over by the following morning.

The Jacobites and their bewildered Spanish allies retreated higher and higher into the mountains. A council of war was held at midnight, when the brief darkness of a Highland midsummer night halted operations. The Spaniards, who declared that they could neither live without bread nor make any hard marches through a country so foreign to them, took the sensible decision to surrender. The Highlanders simply melted away into the wilderness of Kintail; peasant guerrillas who could merge into the landscape.

The English losses were 21 men killed and 121 wounded. 274 hungry Spaniards were taken prisoner. They were marched to Inverness, and then shipped to Edinburgh. There were no savage reprisals. A brief four months later the invaders were repatriated to Spain.

One enduring monument to the battle remains. Ever since that June day in 1719, the mountain on the north side of the Bridge of Shiel has been known as Sgurr nan Spainteach – the Peak of the Spaniards.

Bounded by the beautiful sea-lochs of Loch Alsh and Loch Carron, the peninsula of Lochalsh can also claim as its own one of the most attractive villages on the west coast – Plockton. Situated on a sheltered inlet of Loch Carron, with the bay and outer loch teeming with tree-clad islets, this lush little village has palm trees growing in Harbour Street, an exotic testimony to the mildness of its climate.

Like so much of Wester Ross, Plockton suffered heavily from enforced migration in the nineteenth century. Many of the spruce cottages are holiday homes, occupied only

Opposite. At the close of the eighteenth century there were 3000 head of black cattle in Applecross, but in the 1860s Yorkshire landowner Lord Middleton found deer more profitable than crofters. The crofters were cleared to the shore, and the heart of Applecross became a wilderness.

Above. Wardens of the Beinn Eighe Nature Reserve have acquired much valuable information on the pine marten, one of Britain's rarest and most elusive creatures of the wild.

Below. That haughty aristocrat of the wild – the wild cat.

during the summer months, and the resident population has a higher than average proportion of retired professional people from the south.

But in midsummer, when the Plockton regatta is in full swing and the harbour is crowded with yachts and dinghies, the village is the energetic hub of the gregarious social life of Lochalsh. One of the most instructive paradoxes of the west is the fascinating co-existence of the gloomy doctrine of extreme Calvinism with the native-born Highlander's unrivalled capacity for sustained revelry. It would be regarded as an effete concession to alien conventions if a Plockton ceilidh or dance had reached its apogee before dawn.

On the high moorland above the elongated lochside village of Lochcarron – notable for the profusion of roses around its white cottages in summer – the Allt nan Carnan runs through a steep-sided gorge. Seen from the road, it appears a thin line of treetops. Oak, birch, hazel, ash, aspen, rowan, Scots pine, wych elm, bird cherry, goat willow and wild roses abound, providing the Nature Conservancy with a living laboratory.

The Kishorn road wheels westward away from the course of the Allt nan Carnan, snaking towards the sentinel peaks on the sky-line, guardians of the entrance to the Bealach na Bo, The Pass of the Cattle, the precipitous mountain road to the village of Applecross on the far west of the empty peninsula.

At the close of the eighteenth century there were 300 head of black cattle in the district; and where there were cattle there were crofters. In 1792, the Rev. John McQueen, the parish minister, recorded that the tenants of Mac-Kenzie of Applecross were never behind with their rent. But the MacKenzies handed over their vast estate to the Duke of Leeds for £135,000. In the 1860s, the Duke shed Apple-cross to a fellow Yorkshireman, the eighth Lord Middleton, who collected estates the way lesser mortals collect stamps. He was also the owner of estates in Yorkshire, Nottingham-shire, Lincolnshire, Warwickshire and Derby-shire. Although Applecross was Lord Middle-ton's biggest single property, it provided only £1957 out of a total Middleton rent-roll of £54,014 per year. Deer were more profitable than crofters and their cattle, and Lord Middle-ton lost no time in clearing the crofters from their grazing lands. The heart of Applecross became a wilderness, strictly preserved as a deer forest.

Opposite. Herring boats sheltering from the fury of a
sudden western storm at Gairloch.

Above. There is a rich harvest being reaped from forests
planted half a century ago. Thinnings from the
forestry plantations of Dorusduan, Inverinate, Saraig,
Moyle and Ratigan are transported to the pulp mill at
Corpach along one of the most spectacularly scenic
roads in the country.

81

The peaks of Cul Mor and Cul Beag rise above the surrounding lochans.

On the south shore of Loch Kishorn, the ruined mansion of Courthill House has its bleak gaze fixed upon the mountains of Applecross. The gaunt ruin is a suitably skeletal monument to a land whose people had to make way for deer.

The empty wastes of the Applecross peninsula pose in the starkest imaginable form the plaint of the Highland expatriate; man cannot live by scenery alone. It was voiced as far back as 1836 when the Rev. Roderick McRae sought to have the old copper mine at Kishorn reopened to provide employment for the people. But then came the blight of the sporting landlords, and the banishment of the people.

Today, the skeleton of Courthill House looks across the loch at a scene of bustling activity. A strong pulse of energetic life is beating in lonely Loch Kishorn. Under the towering bulk of Sgurr a' Chaorachdain, the Shepherd's Peak, the world's biggest gravity extraction platform – a 400,000-ton colossus – is under construction.

These master oil-production platforms are assembled off Kishorn Island where Captain Boyle's little squadron lay at anchor in the summer of 1719. Tugs and barges shuttle across from Stromeferry, the old terminus of the Dingwall/Skye Railway, feeding the insatiable appetite of the Kishorn site. There has not been such a stir in the place since that memorable Sabbath of 3 June 1885, when Calvinist crofters rioted against railway officials and police, and staged a sit-in on Strome pier and railway station to prevent the running of a Sunday fish special.

Further north, Loch Maree – with its lochside forests and pine-clad islands – is to be found in one of the most serene of all the High-

83

land glens. Overlooked by the distinctive peaks of Slioch and Beinn Eighe, the loch fringes the Beinn Eighe National Nature Reserve, the first of its kind to be established in Britain.

The reserve is part of the old Kinlochewe deer forest, and contains one of the few surviving fragments of the western type of Scots pine forest. The Wood of the Grey Slopes on the shores of Loch Maree has been the site of a woodland for centuries. There is a living history in trees; some of the most venerable here were seedlings when Charles Edward Stuart raised his standard at Glenfinnan on 19 August 1745.

Wardens of the Beinn Eighe Nature Reserve carry on a programme of continuous study of plants and animals in the reserve. They have acquired much valuable information on the pine marten, one of Britain's rarest creatures of the wild, and one, oddly enough, not under any preservation order. The work of these whole-hearted enthusiasts in providing a greater understanding of the ecology of the Highlands is worthy of far greater recognition.

The 26,827-acre Inverpolly Reserve lies ten miles north of Ullapool. Created by the inspired diktat of the British Fishery Associa-

tion in 1788, Ullapool has now become the main terminal of the car-ferry service from Stornoway in the Isle of Lewis. Holiday-makers need no longer remain shore-bound as the fishing boats put to sea. They can take their cars with them and cross the Minch to the Long Island.

The district of Coigach in which the Inverpolly Reserve is set covers terrain as rugged as any in the Highlands. It is the home of the wild cat and pine marten, fox and badger, otter and ermine, buzzard and golden eagle, ptarmigan and raven, dipper and diver, ring ouzel and the elusive greenshank.

Inverpolly Forest is flanked by three peaks – Cul Beag, Stac Polly and Cul Mor – and a road threads a way through the remote heart of Coigach beyond a string of freshwater lochs to the coast, where the Rhu More peninsula thrusts into the Minch. Stac Polly's sandstone crest – easily climbed – affords a commanding vantage point to survey the mountains, straths, lochs and multitude of lochans of this precious reserve of wildlife.

The Summer Isles can be reached by motor launch from the village of Achiltibuie. Tanera Mor, Tanera Beag, Horse Island and Priest Island all swarm with bird-life. They are

breeding grounds for the heron, shelduck, eider, greylag goose, storm petrel, fulmar, snipe and cormorant.

When Osgood Mackenzie started to create his garden in 1862, the only tree growing on the windswept Inverewe peninsula was a dwarf willow. Today, Inverewe is a resplendent oasis of colour. Tropical plants thrive in profusion, but the Inverewe rhododendrons must rank as the greatest glory of the garden. Yellow and scarlet, red-brown and luscious cream, white and purple and pink, they are a glowing memorial to the dedicated work of a truly great gardener.

From the heights of Mam Ratagan and wild Kintail to the brave headland of Rhu Coigach breasting the waters of the Minch, Wester Ross spells freedom from urban bondage.

There is the Corrieshalloch Gorge, a stupendous, mile-long chasm, one of nature's wonders; gentle Shieldaig on the shores of Loch Torridon; the curving sweep of Gairloch's sandy bay; the high road to Diabaig through the Bealach na Gaoithe, the Pass of the Wind, chasing the setting sun down to the western sea.

More than enough for even the most jaded to gain fresh life and heart.

Opposite. Loch Carron, flanking the northern shore of the Lochalsh peninsula.

Above. Situated on a sheltered inlet of Loch Carron, with the bay and outer loch teeming with tree-clad islets, the little village of Plockton has few peers in the west.

EASTER ROSS

Opposite. Beauly Firth. Above. The fertile Black Isle.

Those who envisage the Highlands as a beautiful wilderness of mist-wreathed mountains, gaunt rock faces, desolate moors and lonely lochs would be confounded by Easter Ross. It is the two-faced joker in the Highland pack. Despite the looming bulk of Ben Wyvis – and for all its 3433 feet the mountain is a benign giant, easily climbed by young and old alike – the peninsulas of Easter Ross comprise the fertile lowlands of the Scottish Highlands. Store cattle come here from the sparse pastures of the west for fattening; lambs for wintering.

This is one of the finest farming areas in Great Britain, the broad fields yielding bumper crops of grain and potatoes. With its leafy hedgerows, well-ordered woodlands, rich arable land, snug with farmhouses that have their roots deep in the soil, and trimly compact little towns, Easter Ross has an air of relaxed well-being more commonly associated with the softer south than the far north of the Highlands.

The verdant peninsula bounded by the Moray and Cromarty Firths is called the Black Isle. There are various explanations for so unlikely a name, the most reasonable being that the peninsula is seldom covered in snow, the land remaining black throughout the winter.

The Black Isle is a green and pleasant land, well endowed with wild flowers, brightened by the gaudy splashes of colour made by its abundant broom and whin, and famed for the extravagant pink of its many sandy bays.

The old walls of Fortrose Cathedral witnessed the trial of Coinneach Odhar, the Brahan Seer, whose book of apocalyptic prophecies is still read avidly in the Highlands, and is in constant demand in all the public libraries. Fortrose Town Hall houses a portrait of the formidable Isabella, Lady Seaforth, who was so little influenced by the Seer's occult powers that she had him put to death by burning.

The waters off Fortrose once sheltered Admiral Byng's Navy, gathered to protect the flank of the Duke of Cumberland's army as it marched on Culloden Moor to crush the last challenge of the Jacobites. Those safe waters are now the playground of the Chanonry Sailing Club.

The little fishing village of Avoch (pronounced 'A'ach') is a curious oddity in this predominantly farming district. With its narrow streets – named after the Mackenzie lairds and their ladies – standing gable-end to the sea, Avoch has an atmosphere entirely its own. This enclave of fisher-folk has preserved down the years a pattern of unusual surnames peculiar to Avoch.

Cromarty, on the tip of the peninsula where the North and South Sutars guard the entrance to the Cromarty Firth, was a thriving port in the days when all coastal communication was by sea. It also had the distinction of being the county town until the counties of Ross and Cromarty were combined in the local government reorganization of 1891. Now Ross and Cromarty in turn vanishes within the vast Highland Region.

Cromarty holds one unique record. It is doubtful if any other comparable small town in such an isolated backwater has produced two internationally renowned figures of such extraordinary diversity as Sir Thomas Urquhart and Hugh Miller.

Born in 1611, and knighted by Charles I in 1641, the peacock figure of Sir Thomas Urquhart cloaked a man of many parts. The

Town houses, Cromarty.

Above. The broad fields yield bumper crops of grain and potatoes.

Opposite. The rich arable lowlands of the Scottish Highlands.

Lord Baron of Cromarty's attributes were legion. Wit, classicist, linguist, mathematician, translator and – most engaging of all – the irrepressible confounder of creditors. He was taken prisoner at Worcester, and had his estates forfeited by Cromwell in 1651, but overcame such misfortunes – and the relentless pursuit of his creditors – with rare panache. This ardent royalist wrote a *'Treatise on Trigonometry'*, devised a universal language in 1653, and produced his classic translation of Rabelais. The precise date of his death is as uncertain as that of his birth, but he went out on a high note. The translator of Rabelais died abroad, reputedly from an excess of joy at the restoration of Charles II.

Hugh Miller was cast in a different mould. Born in 1802, the son of the skipper of a small sloop engaged in the coastal trade, he was only five years of age when his father died at sea. After a spell in a dame school and the Cromarty parish school, the boy became an apprentice stonemason. Labouring in the quarries of Cromarty, he developed an interest in geology, although his first publication was a book of verse, *'Poems written in the Leisure Hours of a Journeyman Mason.'* Exchanging his mason's chisel for a pen, he became a bank accountant in his native town; surely the first – and last – stonemason/banker in Great Britain. Gaining wider notice by his written works, he was summoned to Edinburgh in 1840 to edit the *Witness* newspaper. His geological treatise, *'The Old Red Sandstone'*, which brought him international recognition as a geologist, first

appeared in the columns of the *Witness*. Other works followed, including his evocative *'The Cruise of the Betsy'*, widely read to this day despite its horrific sub-title; *'A Summer Ramble Among The Fossiliferous Deposits Of The Hebrides.'*

Exhausted by his work as editor of the *Witness*, and his searing involvement in the protracted controversy over the disruption of the Kirk, Hugh Miller shot himself on Christmas Eve 1856. The thatched cottage in which he was born in Cromarty has been restored by the National Trust and is open to the public as a museum devoted to his life and work.

Only a decade ago, Cromarty seemed to be doomed to inevitable decline; a decaying backwater by-passed by the modern world. But a thriving Crafts Centre has successfully infused the town with new life and the 'ghost-town' atmosphere is no more.

Cromarty can be seen as the restoration of the old, whereas the north shore of the firth bears the brash imprint of a giant stride into the future. Invergordon – moribund after its abandonment as a major naval base at the end of the First World War – has awakened from the slumbers of half a century.

During that war it had become a huge repair base for the Royal Navy. Between August 1914 and August 1919, 1070 special trains steamed into Invergordon from the south with military supplies. In January 1918, Dalmore, four miles from the town, became US Naval Base No. 17. The Americans were there to aid the British in laying a gigantic minefield, the

Above. Highland One leaves Nigg on passage to the Forties Field.

Below. The first of the steel leviathans takes shape.

Opposite left. The peacock figure of Sir Thomas Urquhart cloaked a man of many parts.

Opposite right. The Pump Room in Strathpeffer still retains its sulphurous aroma.

Northern Barrage, designed to stretch from the Orkneys to the coast of Norway. But the November armistice brought that colossal project to an abrupt end.

Invergordon became a forgotten town until 1968, when 2000 construction workers started building a giant smelter. Thirty months later the smelter was completed and in production. The gleaming Invergordon aluminium smelter, one of the most advanced in Europe, owes much to the vision of Lord Kelvin who sited his pioneer plant at Foyers, less than 30 miles away.

By a strange quirk of fate, the Americans are back, not far from the old US Naval Base No. 17. A Texan construction company have linked with a British firm to form Highland Fabricators of Nigg. Their graving dock at Nigg was dubbed the biggest man-made hole in the world, until the advent of Kishorn.

In August 1974, the first steel leviathan – Highland One – was floated out of the graving dock, and towed through the Sutars on passage to the Forties Field. The 16,000-ton, 460 feet-long 'jacket' section was manoeuvred into position over the drilling spot in 420 feet of water, 105 miles east of the Aberdeenshire coast; the first major contribution from Easter Ross to Scotland's newest industry.

Dingwall, the old county town, is outwardly unaffected by the frenetic activity of the oil-boom. Situated at the junction of the valley of Strathpeffer with the fertile lands around the mouth of the River Conon, it still reflects the life-style of agricultural Easter Ross. Invaded by tweedy farmers every market day, stolid Dingwall needs more than the sight of a Texan oil-man's helmet to change its image.

Dingwall's elegant near neighbour, Strathpeffer – the name is derived from the Gaelic for the valley of the fair river, the Peffery, which rises on the lower slopes of Ben Wyvis – presents an altogether different face to the world.

Splendidly situated in an amphitheatre of green hills, Strathpeffer is one of Scotland's few spas. Its fame dates back to the eighteenth century when local inhabitants discovered the healing properties of its sulphur and chalybeate waters. The most powerful of the numerous springs in the area were tapped, and the trek to Strathpeffer Spa to take the waters began, gaining increasing momentum as Victorian technology opened up the Highlands.

In 1865, powers were granted to extend the railway from Dingwall to Kyle of Lochalsh. The line was to have served Strathpeffer, but Sir William MacKenzie of Coul House obdurately refused to allow the railway to cross his lands. Not only did this deprive the spa of a railway station in a central position, but the new route had to surmount the steep gradient of a four-mile climb to the Raven Rock Summit. Sir William's was a Pyrrhic victory; he died before the line from Dingwall to Strome Ferry was opened in August 1870.

But the growth in popularity of Strathpeffer as a spa made the construction of a branch line inevitable, and the spa acquired a line of its own, and a handsome little station, in June 1885. Since the branch line was axed in 1951, the station building – a gem of Victoriana – has suffered a melancholy decline. Sad to say, no local Betjeman has sprung to its defence.

The English gentry, American industrial

barons, European nobility and the nouveau-riche flocked to take the waters. Victorian guide-books treated the subject at length, and with becoming gravity; *'The two waters chiefly drunk are the Upper Well (a saline sulphur water), mildly purgative and alterative, and the Strong Well, a powerful sulphur water, without any considerable purgative quality. These differences, as at Harrogate, are of great practical value, and it is well therefore before drinking to consult the resident physician. The springs flow through a bituminous rock, to which their qualities are generally attributed, and rise immediately under and around the pump-room, a handsome building prettily situated at the west end of the village. In addition to the saline and sulphur wells, there is a somewhat unique effervescent chalybeate water. This is much used in the season (May to October) as a tonic, the presence of free carbonic acid gas making it an easily digestible as well as most palatable dose. The sulphur waters are recommended in gout, especially in its chronic and irregular forms, in most rheumatic affections, and in disorders of the liver and stomach and skin. Among the latter chronic exzema holds a very important place. The outward use of the water in the form of baths has been greatly developed.'*

The contemporary wisdom is that a pint of the waters will cure even a king-size hangover.

The boundless confidence of the Victorians is enshrined in that monumental edifice the Highland Hotel, rearing over the open centre of the village like a stranded dreadnought. The hotel's imposing balcony – at a conservative estimate the length of several cricket pitches – is capped by pagoda-like towers. The splendid Highland is matched by the Ben Wyvis Hotel. The aptly named Ben Wyvis rivals the mountain in bulk. It was conceived on such a grand scale that the entrance drive could serve as a training track for Marathon runners. On the terraced slopes of the green amphitheatre, flotillas of solid Victorian mansions vie with one another in size and singularity. There is a mannered elegance about Strathpeffer that is uniquely its own.

The leaded-windowed Pump Room still stands, retaining its sulphurous aroma, close by the Spa Pavilion. Not the original Pavilion where the Victorians enjoyed *'spacious accommodation for balls, concerts and refreshments'*, but an equally spacious newcomer where 800 dancers can take the floor.

A mile north of Strathpeffer there is one of the homeliest little castles in Scotland, Castle Leod, ancestral seat of the Earl of Cromarty. It is rumoured that cricket is played in the grounds; one of the lesser known eccentricities of the folk of Easter Ross.

Tain should not be missed. With its tolbooth in the centre of the town, and medieval tower housing the curfew bell, small wonder it was the favourite of King James IV. Tain traces its history back to 1066, and claims to be the oldest royal burgh in Scotland.

For those with a taste for the offbeat there is Fyrish Hill, bearing a replica of the Gates of Negapatam on the summit. This extraordinary monument was built in 1782 by General Sir Hector Munro of Novar to provide employment, and commemorate his relief of the city in the Indian campaign.

Easter Ross can justly claim to be the joker in the Highland pack, proof positive that there is no Highland stereotype. All that is predictable – and that is the great charm of the region – is its baffling, bewildering unpredictability.

SUTHERLAND

Assynt, embodying the very heart and essence of the west.

Sutherland, the South Land of the Norsemen, puts into acute Highland perspective the view of Britain as a grossly overcrowded country. Shout 'overcrowded' in the empty glens, and wait for the mocking echo. Sutherland has space and plenty to spare.

The vast hinterland of its far north west, extending to the awesome buttress of the Clo Mor sea-cliffs near Cape Wrath and lonely Fionn Loch under the primeval hump of Suilven, is a land largely bereft of people. The ruthless Sutherland Clearances of the last century swept the crofters from their townships in the interior and replaced them with huge flocks of sheep – no more docile than the crofters, but infinitely more profitable.

Mountains, lochs and glens of unrivalled beauty sharpen the poignant sight of scattered mounds of stones, graveyards of the once populous crofting townships.

Sutherland spans the breadth of Scotland, providing visual proof positive that the Highland Line is an east/west one, not the north/south line of popular imagination. The cosily domesticated eastern coastal plain, dotted with attractive small towns, is no more kin to the magnificently wild north west than Cumbernauld is to Carloway.

Bonar Bridge, perched on the Kyle, provides a picturesque gateway to Sutherland. The gallant Montrose was defeated near here in 1650 by a Commonwealth army under General Leslie. Montrose escaped to the north by swimming the Kyle, but only postponed the day when he was to be dragged to Edinburgh in chains, doomed to execution.

The road through Bonar Bridge around the Dornoch Firth has become the summer Mecca of family holidaymakers bound for Dornoch with its miles of sand and safe bathing.

The old county town and royal burgh of Dornoch was the seat of the Bishop of Sutherland and Caithness in pre-Reformation days, and consequently enjoyed the status of being one of Scotland's fourteen cities. The Bishop's Palace was burned to the ground in 1570 by a marauding band under the joint command of the Master of Caithness and Mackay of Strathnaver, brigands whose lust for loot outweighed whatever religious scruples they may have possessed.

Dornoch Cathedral was built by Gilbert de Moravia, who was bishop from 1223 to 1245. Reconstructed by the Sutherland family as a parish church in 1835, the cathedral now consists of chancel, nave, transepts and a short central tower crowned with a stunted spire. It was a near kinsman of Gilbert, Andrew de Moravia, who raised the magnificent minster of Elgin.

Dornoch's historic cathedral is not its only distinction. The royal burgh bears an honoured name in the annals of golf. The game was first played here in 1616, and the Royal Dornoch High Course is renowned the world over. A 'new' course was laid out in 1886 by the famous Tom Morris of St Andrews.

Golspie is another favourite resort of the golfing family man, who can indulge himself on the course, while the children have the freedom of the safe sands.

Golspie's chief distinction lies in it being the seat of the Duke of Sutherland's nineteenth-century Ruritanian extravaganza, Dunrobin Castle. Largely the work of Sir Charles Barry – whose pseudo-gothic Houses of Parliament constitute an equally eye-catching confection – Dunrobin was accurately described by a scrupulous Victorian chronicler as being *'a mass of masonry about 100ft square by*

80ft in height, springing from terraced basements, and pierced with rows of oriel and plain windows, ornamented with varied tabling, forming an extensive and imposing frontage to the sea, over which rises a series of lofty towers at the angles of the large square mass, while the whole edifice is crowned by numerous turrets and minarets.' The castle is watched over by the stony stare of the first duke, whose larger than life statue crowns the improbably named Ben Bhraggie.

The original castle is said to have been founded by Robert, Thane of Sutherland – hence the name Dunrobin – in the year 1098. William, the second earl, blessed with the inestimable assets of acumen and longevity, was the shrewd operator who established the base for the grandeur to come. He was one of the Scots nobles who attended the parliament of Alexander III at Scone, when the succession to the crown was settled. William swore fealty to Edward I in 1296, but later threw in his lot with Robert the Bruce, and was one of the eighteen Highland chiefs who fought with Bruce at Bannockburn in the defeat of the English on 24 June 1314. He died in 1325, having held the title, which he inherited at the age of five, for the incredible span of 77 years.

John, the tenth earl, despite the manifold advantages secured for him by the guile and exertions of his predecessors, was a born loser. Getting off to a good start, he accompanied Queen Mary to France in 1550, and was invested with the Order of St Michael. Five years later, he added to his estates by acquiring the Earldom of Ross from the Queen Regent, only to hazard all by joining Huntly's abortive rebellion. His estates were forfeited, and he withdrew to Flanders until the heat was off. In 1567, the forfeiture was rescinded. But the

Opposite. All roads in Sutherland converge on Lairg, scene of Scotland's biggest one-day lamb sale.

Above left. The Victorian traveller could journey from Culrain to Invershin – third class, single – for a halfpenny, the lowest fare on the old Highland Railway.

Above right. A ducal licence to dig for gold.

Above. Crofters were cleared from the best of the arable and grazing lands to make way for sheep.

Opposite. Dunrobin Castle, a modest enough dwelling for a man who in 1874 owned 1,176,343 of the County of Sutherland's 1,297,253 acres.

tenth earl's triumphant return was short-lived. He and his Countess were poisoned by Isobel Sinclair, wife of his uncle, Gordon of Gartay.

Women have played a prominent part in the history of the line. The twelfth earl, Alexander, divorced his wife, Barbara Sinclair, and married Lady Jean Gordon, daughter of the fourth Earl of Huntly. She had in turn been divorced by Bothwell in order to clear the way for his marriage to Queen Mary.

The linking of the dynasty with the English landed aristocracy was brought about by Elizabeth, Countess of Sutherland. She succeeded to the title when little more than a year old. Scottish male chauvinism at once reared its didactic head in the shape of Sir Robert Gordon of Gordonstoun. Sir Robert contested Elizabeth's right to the succession on the grounds that the title could not legally descend to a female heir. The House of Lords, after protracted legal wrangling, decided in her favour on 21 March 1771. The Countess married George Granville Leveson Gower, Viscount of Trentham in September 1785. His Lordship was created Duke of Sutherland in January 1833, but died in July of the same year. The Duchess – thereafter styled Duchess-Countess – almost matched the record of her

ancestor William, the second earl, holding the earldom for three-score years and twelve.

The nineteenth century marked the apogee of the House of Sutherland. The ducal property then extended from Dornoch in the east to Cape Wrath and Tongue in the west. In 1874, according to the Owners of Land (Scotland) Return, the Duke of Sutherland owned 1,176,343 of the County of Sutherland's 1,297,253 acres.

The haughtiest Spanish grandee could not have faulted the Sutherland life-style. The Duke had his own private station at Dunrobin, at which trains called by request to pick up or set down passengers for the castle.

Given such a background, perhaps Dunrobin Castle is not such an extravaganza after all; merely a relatively modest acknowledgement of the singular position of a man who owned an entire county.

Brora, a few miles north of Golspie, is surely the most attractive 'industrial' small town in Scotland. It has the unique distinction for a little Highland town of a golf course designed by one of golf's immortals, the great James Braid. If that isn't attraction enough, Brora has mile upon mile of sands, a famous salmon river and one of the best sea trout lochs

in the country, plus good, small hotels.

The woollen mill continues to export its products throughout the world. And the one certainty, in an ever more uncertain world, is that the distillery, which has been producing fine whisky since 1819, will live to celebrate its bi-centenary.

At Helmsdale, further north, the railway line to Wick and Thurso plunges inland, following the course of the Helmsdale river up Strath Ullie before swinging east at Forsinard. Helmsdale, situated at the mouth of the salmon-fishing river, was a thriving port when the herring fishing was booming. But it is worthy of note for an even more colourful episode in its history. It was at Strath Ullie – ironically enough the last Highland glen to be depopulated under the Clearances – that the Great Sutherland Gold Rush took place.

Nobody knows who first discovered gold deposits in the glen. It may have been the Picts; the remains of their settlements can still be seen in the area, and their craftsmen worked in gold. Or the invading Norsemen. There are two peculiarly shaped, grass-grown mounds in Strath Ullie which, according to local legend, are the burial place of Viking longboats.

But it was in 1868 that a Caithness man by the name of Gilchrist, who had worked as a gold prospector in Australia, decided that there was gold to be panned in the Sutherland hills. Gilchrist and his associates obtained a mining license from the Sutherland Estate – Fee, £1 per month per miner. Subject to the payment of the Crown Royalty, the holder was authorized *'to dig and search for Gold for his own use and behoof, in the alluvial deposit along the sides of the Kildonan, Suisgill and Torish Burns in the Parish of Kildonan.'*

In a matter of weeks, hundreds of diggers were at work. A large tented encampment sprang up where the Suisgill meets the Gold Burn at a spot known to this day as Carnnam-Buth, Place of the Tents. Before long, the tented camp had been buttressed by a long row of wooden shacks, a general store and eating house along the north bank of the Kildonan burn. It was aptly named Baile-an-Or, the Place of Gold.

Despite their lack of experience, it is on record that the gold-miners washed nuggets and flakes of gold to the value of £12,000 in the period 1868–9. In those days, gold fetched only £3 17s an ounce, and it is a reasonable assumption that not all the gold the miners panned was officially declared.

Opposite. Suilven, The Sugar Loaf.

Above. The eroded ridge of Suilven, rearing like the primeval hump of a gigantic stranded dinosaur.

One man who did not share the general euphoria was the Duke of Sutherland. The sight of hundreds of voracious prospectors swarming over his land was not conducive to the ducal peace of mind. His Grace abruptly forbade any more prospecting. The miners were compelled to pack their gear, strike their tents, uproot their shanty town and quit.

In the following years, a great many gold-poachers panned the burns, scooped the banks and dug and smashed rocks. Despite being continually chased off, they returned again and again, braving the interdicts that were taken out against them. Sporadic 'poaching' has never entirely ceased.

The rich mother lodes which shed gold into the streams have never been discovered. Recent geological surveys have stressed the need for a detailed assessment of the area to determine whether hydraulic sluicing techniques along the north-eastern tributaries of the Helmsdale river would be an economic proposition. But any dredging operations would inevitably meet with opposition from the proprietors of the salmon fishings. If there is gold in them thar hills, it is also very much in evidence in the lucrative salmon fishings.

All roads in Sutherland converge on Lairg

Opposite top left. Spring heather burning.

Opposite top right. The soft tranquillity of Loch Assynt.

Opposite bottom. Storm clouds gather near Durness.

Above top. Kyle of Durness where the road sweeps down to the incomparable west.

Above left. A land bereft of people.

Above right. Breaking seas at Clashnessie Bay, near Rhu Stoer.

Scarred by aeons of wind and weather, the buttress of Ben Hope.

at the south-eastern end of Loch Shin. Lairg's annual bonanza occurs in August, when it is the scene of the biggest one-day lamb sale in Scotland.

Farmers, crofters, shepherds – and their dogs – congregate from all over the Highlands. Curiously enough, the scene recalls those nineteenth-century gatherings when the faithful trekked long distances on foot to hold communion services on the open hillside. There is the same communal concentration on the one central figure, only at the Lairg Sale it is the auctioneer, not the minister, and almost all the communicants have travelled in comfort by car.

The faces around the sale ring exemplify non-urban man. They are canny faces. Faces well aware that 100 pence make £1, but that good stock cannot be measured in merely monetary terms. They are the same faces that Peter Breughel painted more than 400 years ago.

Downstream from Lairg, the River Shin sweeps through thickly wooded gorges, browses in dark pools, and foams through the gap between high rock walls before cascading down in the spectacular Falls of Shin. There is no better vantage point to observe the graceful strength of the salmon, arching high in the air as they fight their way upstream to the spawning grounds through the seething heart of the falls.

Across the river from Invershin (prior to 1 January 1917, a third-class ticket from Invershin to Culrain cost one halfpenny, the lowest fare on the Highland Railway), stands the most extraordinary Youth Hostel in the entire country: Carbisdale Castle, a frothy confection straight from the pages of a Ruritanian romance.

This baroque fantasy demands lights, cameras, clapperboard and an old-style Hollywood director armed with eye-shade, three-foot cigar and loud-hailer. He would be marshalling a cast of thousands, all in period costume.

Carbisdale Castle was built by a Dowager Duchess of Sutherland, and was not completed until 1914; a final fling before Edwardian exuberance was extinguished in the bleak khaki realities of the First World War.

The road north from Lairg thrusts across the solitary wastes of the high moors to the majestic sweep of the Kyle of Tongue, skirting the shores of remote Loch Eriboll and winding through Durness of the famous Smoo Cave.

Never was there a name – derived from the old Norse *smuga*, meaning a narrow cleft – less suited to its subject. This huge cavern, like caves in Islay, Colonsay, Mull and Skye, has its story of the disappearing piper. But in the Cave of Smoo, with its dark inner caverns and hidden waterfall, the story is all too believeable.

A new aspect of Durness is the Balnakeil Craft Village, where a group of craftsmen – and women – have transformed the ugly site of an old radar station into a centre of the creative arts. Whatever else, the potters, wood-carvers and painters cannot complain that the urban world is too much with them at Balnakeil.

Durness is the northernmost apex of the road; the point where it wheels south to explore the incomparable west.

West Sutherland is the place that dreams are made of. A coastline pierced by the sea, with the road hugging the contours of the hill, every bend revealing a new, unexpected vista; bays and lochs studded with islets; the air of such a sparkling clarity of light that every ridge and corrie on distant hills is etched razor-sharp. A land of bewildering changes of mood; a tempestuous, storm-laden sky hurling fierce black rainclouds on the hills, only for them to vanish as quickly as they formed, and the entire panoramic spread of hill and loch and sea to emerge miraculously new-born under a radiant blue sky innocent of rain.

On a still evening, with the fishing fleet gathered in around the pier under the high hills, few places can match the serenity of Kinlochbervie on Loch Inchard. Four miles

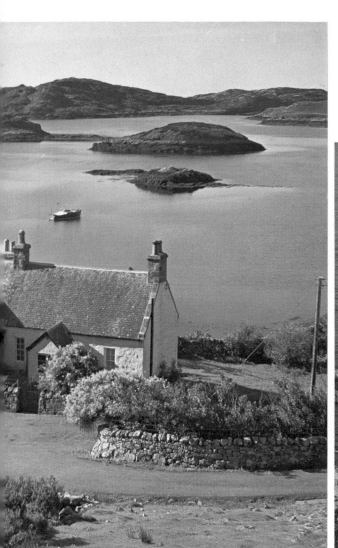

Opposite. Eddrachillis Bay, studded with innumerable green and rocky islets.

Above. Handa Island, abandoned during the great potato famine of the 1840s, and now a bird sanctuary. Guillemots, kittiwakes and razorbills abound.

beyond Kinlochbervie is the little township of Sheigra. Another four miles on foot across the moor – and no walk in all Scotland ends with a richer reward – takes the traveller to the splendour of Sandwood Bay.

Such a solitude enfolds Sandwood Bay it seems as if the sands could never before have taken the imprint of a human foot. But seven centuries ago, the war-fleet of a Norse king rounded stormy Cape Wrath and dropped anchor off-shore. To the salt-rimmed eyes of the Vikings such a landfall after a waste of sea must have been in the nature of a miracle, as if the forecourt of Valhalla lay before them.

The Kylesku Ferry – one of the few free vehicular ferries in Great Britain – sets the traveller ashore in a district embodying the very heart and essence of the west – Assynt.

Take the winding road west through Drumbeg, past tiny lochans thick with waterlillies, opening on to vistas of Eddrachillis Bay, studded with innumerable green and rocky islets, to Stoer and the exhilarating sweep down to Lochinver.

It is a road to daunder along, and savour at leisure.

Above. The Stoer Light faces a waste of sea.

Opposite. Sand patterns on the Kyle of Tongue under
brooding Ben Loyal.

CAITHNESS

Opposite. The famous John O'Groats. Above. The open Caithness road.

Although Caithness embraces the most northerly corner of the Scottish mainland, it is the least 'Highland' in character of all the component parts of the Highland Region. It is a reasonably safe bet that more Gaelic is spoken in Cambridge, England – if only by expatriate Highland academics. Caithness was never part of the *Gaidhealtachd*, the western enclave where Gaelic is still the cherished mother tongue of the bulk of the native population. Most of the place names in this northern redoubt are of Norse origin, significant pointers to the pervasive influence of those early raiders and settlers from across the northern sea.

Caithness – a blunt triangle of moors, lochs and surprisingly fertile farmland – is bounded by the Atlantic Ocean, the Pentland Firth and the North Sea.

The soaring heads of Dunnet, Duncansby, Holborn and Noss afford spectacular watching-points for the teeming bird-life of the cliffs. At Bochailean, south west of Berriedale, close to the Sutherland border, there is a huge settlement of kittiwakes, estimated at 10,000 pairs, and the biggest breeding colony of cormorants in Scotland nests near the Ord of Caithness.

Until 1811, when the first road edged tentatively into Caithness, the only access was by sea. As if in deference to the past, the main trunk roads hug the coast, never straying far from the sea. Entry from Sutherland across the formidable granite promontory of the Ord of Caithness poses no hazards today.

Only 63 years after the first road had made its belated way north, the railway from Helmsdale to Wick and Thurso was opened to public traffic. The line enters Caithness four miles east of Forsinard, and the bleak, exposed moors across the border from Sutherland were soon tagged 'The Country of the Snow Drifts' by Victorian railwaymen. For all the contemporary grumbles about the weather, their arctic winters are rarely experienced nowadays.

The herring season was at its peak when the atrocious winter of 1894–5 laid icy hands on Caithness. Getting the fish trains through from Wick to the markets in the south became a test of endurance. On one occasion, after being abandoned by its crew in a raging blizzard that had formed deep drifts, a fish special was completely buried at the inappropriately named Fairy Hillocks near Altnabreac. When the train was dug out ten laborious days later, the herring were found to be in perfect condition. The deep snow had acted as a giant deep-freeze.

The royal burgh and old county town of

Wick has a languid air, as if it is still drawing breath after the frantic exertions of the last century. Those exertions were centred upon the harbour; the focal point of the great herring-boom with its golden promise of an endless Eldorado.

The harbour was built at an enormous capital cost, but the breakwater was wrecked by a terrible storm during the winter of 1871. The damage was estimated at £140,000; an enormous sum to be borne by a small town on the northernmost tip of the Scottish mainland. It is an indication of the wealth in the herring-fishing industry that the money was found.

At the height of the fishing, a vast fleet of 700 boats crowded into Wick Harbour. Gaelic-speaking islanders from the west invaded the town; the men to help man the boats, and the women to work at the herring-curing stations. Working outside on the quays in crews of three, two gutting and one packing, the girls sang as they worked, hard at it from six in the morning until late at night. Small wonder that the now somnolent harbour is heavy with an aura of the past. The ghosts are palpable.

But Wick still has its thrusting innovators. The town houses the first new glass factory to

Opposite left. Seen against the elemental rocks and sea of the northernmost corner of the Scottish mainland, the science-fiction steel containment sphere is a jolting reminder that nuclear technology has broken new frontiers far removed from the old industrial battlegrounds.

Opposite right. Armed with their immensely long, medieval blowing irons, they are the sorcerer's apprentices come triumphantly to life.

be built in Scotland this century.

One of the fascinations of glass is that the system of manufacture has remained largely unchanged for more than a thousand years. Silica sand, the basic raw material, comes from Loch Aline in Argyll; a source only discovered during the last war. After the sand has been dried in electric sifters, chemicals are added. Absolute accuracy in the mix is so essential that an apothecary's scales are used in measuring the chemicals.

The first step in the manufacturing process is the placing of an empty clay pot in a pot arch – a furnace designed to pre-heat the pot; the temperature being raised gradually to 1400° Centigrade over a period of seven days.

The hand-made clay pot, which has a capacity of twenty cwt, is then transferred to a furnace. The incandescent pot, glowing bright

orange, is hauled out of the pot arch on a giant toasting fork and trundled across to a furnace. A batch of the mix is shovelled into the pot on long shovels, and the mix is melted down into molten glass.

What the visitors come to see – and they flock to the Caithness Glass Factory in their tens of thousands every summer – are the glass-blowers at work. Young boys; locals all. Armed with their immensely long, medieval blowing irons, they are the sorcerer's apprentices come triumphantly to life.

On the cliffs near Noss Head north of Wick, the ruins of the adjoining medieval castles of Girnigoe and Sinclair face the sea. These former Sinclair strongholds have been so shaped by wind and weather that they have the appearance of natural stacks arising from the storm-ravaged cliffs.

Dunnet Bay, with its miles of smooth, firm sand, has become a popular sand-yachting centre. There are few sights more aesthetically satisfying than that of great spreads of canvas coming alive in the wind, sending the yachts scudding across the broad sweep of the bay; a bay fringed by a crystalline sea and backed by circling green hills.

Perched in lonely splendour high above the bay is the House of the Northern Gate. The house was built for Admiral Sinclair before the First World War. A corner window in the drawing room served as the admiral's spyhole, where he could train his glass on the northern waters. This is the ideal spot for a crow's-nest view of the 'Northern Gate', the Pentland Firth. This formidable sea-gate is barred by the tumultuous Merry Men of Mey, a tidal race that has claimed many a victim.

Opposite. Ceaseless pounding by tumultuous seas have shaped the dramatically rugged Caithness coastline.

Top. Sea fishing trips can be made from any of the numerous small harbours between Scrabster and Lybster.

Bottom left. Detached stacks rise above the waves like stranded keeps.

Above. Soaring Noss Head affords a spectacular observation point for the teeming life of the bird cliffs.

Thurso went through the traumas of instant growth long before the first drilling rig ventured into northern waters in search of oil. With the advent of the Atomic Energy Authority's Dounreay project, the town's population trebled within a decade. But the old and the new have coalesced with surprising ease, and the invigorating atmosphere of Scotland's most northerly mainland town is not solely due to its bracing air.

Some of the most advanced fast reactor technology in the world is being developed on Thurso's doorstep at Dounreay. Even today, when the Dounreay Fast Reactor has long been dwarfed by the gargantuan Prototype Fast Reactor, the DFR retains the capacity to startle.

Seen against the elemental rocks and sea of the northernmost corner of the Scottish mainland, the science-fiction steel containment sphere is a jolting reminder that nuclear technology has created new frontiers far removed from the old industrial battlegrounds.

No traveller should fail to pause at Reay, west of Dounreay, to honour the memory of an obscure cleric and writer, the Rev. Alexander Pope.

The Rev. Pope's sermons have not survived, and his literary works, such as *'Description of the Dune of Dornedilla'*, are known only to the most erudite of Highland bibliophiles. But the Reay minister deserves to be remembered for one of the dottiest literary pilgrimages in history. An admirer of his namesake, the poet Alexander Pope, the Rev. Alexander mounted his pony one summer's day in the year 1732 and rode all the way from Caithness to Twickenham to pay his respects to the poet. Not only did he make the heroic journey down, he survived the return trip to his lonely parish. Happily, a friendship was forged, and the two Alexanders corresponded in later years, maintaining the improbable link between Reay and Twickenham.

Caithness offers a variety of sea-angling – from rock, beach, or boat. Tucked away under the Braes of the Holborn Head, the port of Scrabster is within easy reach of the prolific fishing grounds of the Pentland Firth. Boats and tackle are readily available, and even the tyro may be lucky enough to land a giant halibut. Cod, pollack, skate, mackerel and conger abound, and sea-fishing trips can be made from any of the numerous fishing villages between Scrabster and the little haven of Lybster.

One of the fascinations of Caithness is the

number of tiny fishing coves hidden away at the foot of the great sea-cliffs. Whaligoe, reached by 365 steps cut into the face of the cliff, is a memorial to the tenacity of a people determined to overcome all obstacles in the struggle for survival.

The early summer and autumn runs of sea trout can be seen at Wester River and Thurso River, both noted for their spectacular runs of grilse. Caithness is blessed with more than a hundred inland lochs – all free of coarse fish – and the angler with a penchant for brown trout can afford to be selective.

370 million years ago, most of Caithness was covered by a vast inland sea, known to geologists as Lake Orcadie. The fossils of the long-dead fish in Lake Orcadie are entombed in the Old Red Sandstone of Caithness, waiting, millenia later, to be exposed by the geologist's hammer and chisel.

The fossil fish put man's artefacts into true perspective. In the geological life-span, the 3000 years gap between the construction of the Grey Cairns of Camster and the steel containment sphere at Dounreay is no more than a heartbeat.

Under the big Caithness sky an Olympian view of life comes naturally.

Opposite. From the boatyard at Scrabster, it's down to the sea in concrete ships.

Above. At the height of the herring boom Wick Harbour sprouted a forest of masts. Small wonder that the now somnolent harbour is heavy with an aura of the past, when the *Sea Eagle* and *Nicoline* were fresh from the builders' yards.

117

SKYE

Opposite. The Black Cuillin. Above. Her Majesty's mails safely delivered in Hungladder.

On the evening of Wednesday 1st September 1773, that unlikely twosome Samuel Johnson and James Boswell made their weary way down to the inn at Glenelg. After having struggled up the track and across the high pass by way of Mam Ratagan, the pair of them were tired, fretful and hungry.

Highland hostelries were not noted for an abundance of creature comforts, but the lack of even the most primitive bill of fare at Glenelg Inn incensed the great lexicographer who dearly loved his food. *'Of the provisions,'* he commented acidly, *'the negative catalogue was copious. Here was no meat, no milk, no bread, no eggs, no wine. We did not express much satisfaction.'*

Dr Johnson spent a wretched night sleeping on a bundle of hay, buttoned up in his riding coat. *'Mr Boswell being more delicate,'* the 64-year old sage observed with malice aforethought, *'laid himself sheets with hay over and under him and lay in linen like a gentleman.'*

Kylerhea and the steep slopes of Glen Arroch in Skye – the drove road to the south for the island's black cattle – lay directly across the tidal race of the narrows, but the travellers were bound down the Sound of Sleat to Armadale. It was raining as they boarded a boat and embarked on their pilgrimage to Eilean Sgaithanach, the Winged Isle.

The name reeks of flatulent poesy. But Skye is indeed the Winged Isle. The peninsulas of Sleat and Strathaird, Minginish and Duirinish, Vaternish and Trotternish reach into the waters of the Minch like outspread pinions.

Skye is Skye. Unique. A microcosm of the Highland scene in all its infinite diversity. Subject to lightning changes of mood, switching – at the drop of an oilskin – from a sombre, all-pervading greyness to such a diamond-hard brilliance of light that a tiny figure on a distant hill springs into such startling prominence that the air seems to have acquired a telescopic quality.

On such rare days, it is as if the scales had been peeled from clouded human eyes, giving vision a new dimension. Hills, lochs, sea and sky have such a pristine clarity, it is not too fanciful to imagine that the world has been created anew. Cloud and rain provide the perfect overture for such a stunning metamorphosis.

Kyle of Lochalsh, as the main road and rail terminus, is the most popular jumping-off point for Skye. A few minutes trip across the narrow straits and the car-ferry is nosing alongside the tide-swept jetty beside the green grave of ruined Castle Maoil.

Kyleakin is Acunn or Haco's Strait. On a September evening in the year 1263, the war-fleet of the Norse king slumbered at anchor here, Haco's warriors at ease, unaware that the gods were conspiring against their king.

At the beginning of the hustling nineteenth century, Lord MacDonald of Sleat laid his ambitious plans for the creation of a new town at Kyleakin. With singular insensitivity, even in so pragmatic an age, he christened his grandiose project New Liverpool. Fortunately, all that remains of the scheme is an artist's impression in the form of a contemporary engraving.

Eight miles from Kyleakin, the village of Broadford straggles around its wide bay, overlooked by Beinn na Caillich and the Red Hills. Hugh Miller gently coveted the island of Pabay out in the bay. *'He would be a happy geologist,'* Miller mused, *'who, with a few thousands to spare, could call Pabba his own.'*

The petrifactions of the tiny island's shores

The village of Broadford straggles around its wide bay,
overlooked by Beinn nan Caillich and the Red Hills.

evoked a typically vivid Miller observation. In *'The Cruise of the Betsy'*, he wrote, *'Every rock is a tablet of hieroglyphics, with an ascertained alphabet; every rolled pebble a casket, with old pictorial records locked up within.'*

As in the days of Hugh Miller, Broadford is the ideal centre for forays into the Cuillins and south Skye. The road west from Broadford skirts the Red Hills by Torrin and loops around Loch Slapin. Even the rusting corrugated-iron roof of a byre undergoes a subtle transition in this landscape. It could be an integral part of a Hebridean Shangri-La shielded from the encroachment of the outside world by the mighty pinnacled ridge of Blaven.

The road ends at Elgol near Strathaird Point, the tip of the peninsula nosing out into the Cuillin Sound which separates Loch Slapin from Loch Scavaig.

There is no more wildly theatrical backdrop than the jagged peaks of the Black Cuillins. Seen across Loch Scavaig from Elgol, they look like the ramparts of Valhalla, fit sanctuary for the heroes of Odin.

Coruisk, which so fascinated and repelled the early Victorians, can be reached by motor launch from Elgol or on foot through Glen Sligachan. Another route is by the track around the shore at the head of Loch Scavaig, where the rock obstacle of the 'Bad Step' has to be traversed. Coruisk, the Corrie of Water, is a fine example of the Victorian penchant for extravagant over-dramatization. Variously described as 'grim', 'God-forsaken', 'eerie', 'grotesque' and 'sterile' by eminent contemporary chroniclers, Coruisk of the caressing name has a peculiarly delicate, austere beauty to which the Victorians were strangely blind.

A steep path across the hills from Coruisk leads to Glenbrittle, where rich pastures make it the most fertile glen in the Minginish peninsula. Haunt of climbers, the sandy bay at Glenbrittle mushrooms into a gaily coloured tented town in the summertime.

Sleat presents a surprisingly verdant face of Skye, and there is no better approach than by sea from Mallaig to Armadale.

Neither Johnson nor Boswell warmed to Sir Alexander MacDonald who received them at Armadale. The bleak encounter with old Etonian Sir Alexander doubtless inspired Johnson's magisterial pronouncement; *'Their chiefs being now deprived of their jurisdiction have already lost much of their influence, and as they gradually degenerate from patriarchial rulers to rapacious landlords they will divest themselves of the little that remains.'*

If only Sir James MacDonald, the brilliant elder brother of the aloof Alexander, had been host there would have been a vastly different story to tell of that first encounter on Skye. No man in all the Hebrides was better fitted to pit his wits against the mental gymnastics of Dr Johnson and his ebullient alter ego.

Sir James was 21 and a student at Oxford when Boswell first met him in London. The diarist promptly confided to his journal that he had met *'a remarkable young man of good parts and great application.'* The young MacDonald was already known as the 'Marcellus of the North' because of his phenomenal learning, and he moved in a glittering intel-

Opposite left. Lobster creels decorate the beach at
Harlosh, Loch Bracadale.

Opposite right. Seen across Loch Scavaig from Elgol the
Cuillins could be the ramparts of Valhalla.

Above. An old Black House at Lealt in the cold winter
of its years.

lectual circle. One of his contemporaries who accompanied him on the Grand Tour deemed essential for the education of young gentlemen was Adam Smith, Professor of Moral Philosophy at Glasgow.

On his return to Skye, Sir James turned his considerable talents to the improvement of his estate. He planned to make Portree a centre of trade and industry, but failing health forced him to seek the sun again. Of all his plans, only the establishment of a school in Portree was achieved in his life time.

During his final illness in Rome, the Pope sent a cardinal to see the young nobleman who had been acclaimed throughout Europe. *'I addressed him in seven different languages,'* the cardinal reported to the Pope, *'and he answered me in all with fluency and obvious familiarity; and when I was about to leave the room he gave an order to his servant in a language that I am sure nobody in the world understands but themselves.'*

Sir James MacDonald died in Rome at the tragically early age of 25. Few men have made such an impact upon their contemporaries given so brief a span of life in which to establish themselves.

The drowsy little crofting townships scattered about the wooded, grassy glades between Ardvasar and the delectable Isle Ornsay - the ebb-tide island – would make the perfect setting for a pastoral period piece on film. But the players would have to be imported. Crofters are thin on the ground in what was once the heartland of the MacDonald grandees.

What an Edwardian writer on Skye aptly termed the Great North Road, runs from Isle Ornsay across the moors to Broadford, swings west by Loch Ainort, thrusts through the hills

124

Left. The Cuillins.

Below. The salmon fishermen of Staffin.

to Sconser and Sligachan and undulates along Glen Varragill to the capital of Skye, Portree.

The distinctive, truncated beacon of Dun Caan is a constant reminder to those taking the Great North Road of the close presence of Raasay, in the waters of the sound, off Skye's eastern shore. Boswell loved Raasay, not least perhaps because the island affords superb vantage points for seeing Loch Sligachan and the Cuillins at their spectacular best. The exuberant Jamie climbed to the summit of the flat-topped Dun Caan, where he celebrated by dancing a reel, and ate *'cold mutton and bread and cheese and drank brandy and punch.'*

Until 1540, Portree was known as Kiltaraglen. In that year, James V anchored his fleet in the landlocked harbour, and exacted homage from the dissident chiefs. Suitably impressed by this display of military muscle, they did a spot of forelock-tugging and swiftly changed the name of the place to Port an Righ, the King's Harbour, and Portree it has remained. As befits a mini-capital, Portree has a healthy conceit of itself. Shopkeepers in the tiny main street have been known to refer to customers from the outlying districts as being 'in from the country.'

Portree lies at the base of the matchless peninsula of Trotternish, which is bisected by the ridged spine of the Storr range and the Quiraing. On the eastern flank, one of Skye's best-known landmarks, the Old Man of Storr, rises 160 feet high from its seemingly precarious perch on the rim of a corrie.

Seen from the little township of Rigg, this weird rock formation assumes the shape of a huge, cowled figure with a tiny head, doomed to face forever north. When the mist smokes around the Storr, the Old Man and his gro-

Above. What Boswell called 'The fine verdure of Raasay'.

Opposite left. The River Lealt plunging down the gorge to the sea at Invertote.

Opposite right. The defiant shell of Duntulm Castle, the ancient seat of the MacDonalds of the Isles.

tesquely shaped henchmen acquire the illusion of movement, like ancient trolls suddenly come to life.

Further north, where the line of hills inclines to the west, the cone-shaped peak of Sgurr a' Mhadaidh Ruaidh, the Hill of the Red Fox, is easily recognizable. The hollow below the hill formed by the drained bed of Loch Cuithir was the unlikely scene of industrial activity in the two decades before the First World War, and enjoyed a brief resurrection in the 1950s.

The hidden Table Rock, high among the crags of the Quiraing, was the most popular tourist attraction of all in Victorian days; a constant stream of carriages taking the road from Uig across the hill to Staffin.

More opulent Victorians arrived in Staffin Bay by steam-yacht. Whilst servants hefted the picnic hampers, indomitable Victorian gentlewomen, triumphing over tight corseting and a plethora of petticoats, toiled up the track to the Needle Rock.

The enormous phallic pinnacle of the Needle Rock screens the entrance to the Table; a smooth stretch of emerald-green turf enclosed by bare rock walls. Clefts in the rock on the eastward side give an aerial view of the little township of Digg far below and the tremendous sweep of the Trotternish coast ranged against the Minch. The peripatetic ex-Empress Eugenie of France was one of the many Victorian notables who made the climb into the green heart of the Quiraing.

The Great North Road, after nearing Rubha Hunish – the most northerly point on the island – dips south, passing close to the storm-swept ridge where the ruins of Duntulm Castle stare forlornly out to sea. The last occupant of this ancient seat of the MacDonalds of the Isles was Domhnull a' Chogaidh, Donald of the Wars. Perhaps the tag was an ironic one, for Domhnull a' Chogaidh features in local lore for his famous Duntulm Ball, at which a clutch of maidens were lustily deflowered.

The road runs through the croftlands of Kilmuir, corkscrews down to the headland-guarded sweep of Uig Bay, and takes a long detour by way of Loch Snizort before swinging west to Vaternish and Duirinish.

Dunvegan lies between the two peninsulas, and owes its fame to the presence of what is reputed to be the oldest inhabited castle in the British Isles. Boswell, disputing with Lady MacLeod – who favoured flitting to a more sylvan site – on the suitability of the rock-girt castle as a home, had evidently drunk himself into a flush of feudal enthusiasm. The young Jamie was delighted when Johnson, all claret and brandy geniality, declared, *'Madam, rather than quit the old rock, Boswell would live in the pit; he would make his bed in the dungeon.'* The dungeon is all that remains of the original fortress. The present building reflects the nineteenth-century taste for ornate, Scots baronial clutter.

Visitors flock to Dunvegan from every

corner of the British Isles and every part of the world. The vastly improved Kyle car-ferries disgorge tens of thousands of cars every summer at Kyleakin. But despite such a colossal annual influx, absolute peace can be found once the roads are left for the moors and the hills. Too much peace perhaps, as in the little glen of Lorgill; the glen of the deer's cry.

A track leads from Ramasaig, a few miles south of Glendale, to this empty glen. It was not always so. In the summer of 1830, a small band consisting of a sheriff officer, four policemen and the minister came to Lorgill. The ten crofting families were summoned. A proclamation was read to them by the sheriff officer; *'To all the crofters in Lorgill. Take notice that you are hereby duly warned that you all be ready to leave Lorgill at twelve o'clock on the 4th August next with all your baggage but no stock and proceed to Loch Snizort, where you will board the ship* Midlothian *(Captain Morrison) that will take you to Nova Scotia, where you are to receive a free grant of land from Her Majesty's Government. Take further notice that any crofter disobeying this order will be immediately arrested and taken to prison. All persons over seventy years of age and who have no relatives to look after them will be taken care of in the County Poorhouse. This order is final and no appeal to the Government will be considered. God Save the Queen.'*

God save us all, they packed their gear obediently and departed. On 4 August 1830, after singing the 100th Psalm, the men, women and children of Lorgill abandoned their homes in the glen and took the long trek over the moors to the emigrant ship in Loch Snizort.

It is in such empty glens that the history, the pathos, the beauty and the lure of Skye strike to the heart.

Top. Sir James MacDonald, the Marcellus of the North.

Bottom. Phallic pinnacle supreme, The Needle Rock.

Opposite. Mighty Blaven of the pinnacled ridge.

WESTERN ISLES

Opposite. The blue hills of Harris. Above. The Standing Stones of Callanish.

Ranged in a splintered arc against the might of the Atlantic Ocean, the Western Isles extend 130 miles from the Butt of Lewis in the north to Barra Head in the south. Lewis, Harris, North Uist, Benbecula, South Uist and Barra, with their satellite isles, constitute the heartland of the *Gaidhealtachd*, the Land of the Gael. Given the harsh imperatives of history, they have become the last major redoubt in Scotland of the Gaelic language.

Paradoxes abound, as they always have. One of the earliest travellers to the Hebrides expressed amazement at the freakish singularity of Lewis and Harris, *'which two although they ioyne be a necke of land ar accounted dyvers Ylands.'* And to this day they have preserved individual identities, as if they were indeed separate islands.

The port of Stornoway in Lewis is the largest town in the Western Isles. Stornoway has an atmosphere compounded of the assurance of the *Leodhasach*, rooted firmly in the belief that his island backyard is the fulcrum of the nation around which lesser bodies – like the Westminster Parliament – make a distant orbit, impinging only rarely upon the island's collective consciousness. There is a driving energy here, unknown in any other Hebridean town, drawing its impetus perhaps from the busy clack of the weavers' looms.

Many of the shopfronts display the familiar names of the nationwide multiple stores, but Stornoway has its own surprising exotica – an enclave of Pakistani trading establishments. Unlike earlier British immigrants, many of these late arrivals have acquired a working knowledge of Gaelic.

But despite the bustle of the crowded streets, the thrusting traffic, the aura of a metropolis in miniature, this is an urban centre with a difference. It is not due solely to the bilingual street signs, strange as it is for those from a monoglot culture to be confronted by *Cromwell Street.* *Sraid Chrombail* The difference lies in the island faces; faces that have retained their individual identity and not been frozen into a mask of urban anonymity. The townsfolk have time to stop and talk; time to greet a friend with the distinctive island salute of a long, lingering handclasp; time to become totally involved in the voluble chat so dear to the heart of the Gaelic-speaking islander.

The Lewis Sabbath sees a total transformation from the weekday bustle. It can best be savoured by taking a walk through the most

westerly rookery in the British Isles in the wooded grounds of Lews Castle. A path leads down to the sea-wall gate below the lodge in the castle grounds. The stone archway, flanked by the interlocking branches of its guardian trees, overlooks the inner harbour where the fishing fleet is at rest, moored for the weekend.

Nothing stirs in the harbour or the surrounding streets. There has been a silent revolution overnight; the noisy tyranny of the internal combustion engine overthrown, its discordant din banished. The quiet is tangible; a refreshment to the senses. All that can be heard is the murmuring slap of the tide against the hulls of the fishing boats, and the cries of the frustrated gulls against the slow tolling of a church bell.

The fishing fleet put to sea in the Monday dawn, nosing out into the Minch between the arms of Arnish Point and Holm Point. The new supply base and fabrication yard at Arnish Point may stem the drift of the vigorous young away from the island. But there is a grim irony in the fact that such a resurgence should be centred on Arnish Point. Arnish looks across to the dread Beasts of Holm, scene of the most terrible tragedy in the history of Lewis.

Opposite. One of the most impressive artefacts of Neolithic man, the Standing Stones of Callanish have defied the ravages of time. These megaliths of unbelievable antiquity dominate the landscape.

Above. Many who lie here had to traverse the world for their daily bread. If they had a wish it would be that those born to the beauty of Barra were enabled to live and work and die on Barra.

133

On the last day of 1918, the Admiralty vessel *Iolaire* steamed out of Kyle of Lochalsh crowded with Lewismen returning from the war. Many of them were within sight of their homes when the *Iolaire* foundered on the rocks of Holm. 205 men perished. New Year's Day 1919 was a day of bitter grief for Lewis. There was not a single township in the island which had not lost someone dear to them. No Lewisman can ever lay eyes on the Beasts of Holm without recalling the loss of the *Iolaire*.

Sixteen miles from Stornoway, across the moors and lochans of the rural hinterland, there is a little west-coast township which bears a name as world-renowned as that of Stonehenge. The Standing Stones of Callanish were described by Martin Martin in 1703 as *'Ye Heathen Temple.'* Whatever the religious purpose in the mysterious symmetry of the megaliths, this austere temple, open to the sky, is one of the most impressive artefacts of neolithic man in the western world.

The great avenue of megaliths with its centre circle of massive stones – the work of a supposedly primitive people – has defied the ravages of time. The stones were standing at Callanish the day the Greeks counted the Persian dead at Marathon; they had with-

stood the Atlantic gales for centuries when Nineveh fell; they were old memorials to old gods when Rome was a nameless huddle of huts fouling the banks of the Tiber – and yet we know nothing of the men who raised them.

But it is when the sun goes down over Loch Roag that the brooding aura of the Standing Stones is at its most potent. They dominate the landscape in the gloaming; awesome shadowy figures of unbelievable antiquity, posing questions far outwith the scope of our primitive computerized gadgetry.

The Callanish road reaches its western apex at Carloway where the magnificent ruin of the Broch of Dun Carloway stands high on a green knoll above the township. The broch reigns benignly over a crofting township deeply rooted in the land of Lewis. The glorious circular symmetry of the inward-sloping wall of the broch is a delicate work of art, the lasting legacy of a pastoral people without a written language. They wrote their history in enduring stone, raising fortress brochs to guard against invaders from the sea.

The crofters of Carloway, like their ancient forbears, take fish from the loch, cut peats from the moor and harvest their crops. Past and present are closely interwoven here, and

Opposite. Thatched cottages of a South Uist crofting township; the complete antithesis of the urban ant-heap.

Above. A stubble of thatch above the crofter's door.

the old broch may yet sight new invaders from the sea – helmeted like the Norsemen, but intent upon plunder the Vikings never knew, the black, black oil below the sea-bed.

There could be no greater contrast to the mini-metropolis of Stornoway than the Uig peninsula – birthplace of Coinneach Odhar, the Brahan Seer – in the south west of Lewis. The tempo of life in little crofting townships like Carnish beats in time to the slow drift of the seasons. There is a precious quiet in this place. It is possible to stand on the curving sweep of Traigh Mangersta, solitary as Crusoe – not even the footprints of a Man Friday in the sand – and feel that the Atlantic rollers are breaking on an undiscovered edge of the world.

But the most striking feature of Lewis is not its abundance of empty beaches, but the density of its rural population. Unlike other Hebridean islands, the croft houses of Lewis crowd together in an almost urban huddle. A Skyeman, accustomed to a thin scatter of houses widely dispersed in straggling townships, would regard the tightly packed Lewis townships as crofting towns. Indeed, from Swanibost in the far north of the island to the Port of Ness, there is virtually one long street of croft houses.

Beyond the sand dunes of Eoropie beach, the Butt of Lewis faces an infinity of ocean and the full frontal assault of the Atlantic. In the beginning, there were the rocks and the sea; and they are still there, fearsome black molars of inshore reefs, pitted by aeons of wind and weather and the relentless pounding of the savage sea. It is the storm-wracked Butt of Lewis, above all, that explains the tenacious attachment of the *Leodhasach* to the sparse soil of his native island.

The boundary between Lewis and Harris follows the line of the high hills between the deep indentations made by Loch Resort in the west and Loch Seaforth in the east. After the undulating moorland of Lewis, mountainous Harris presents a startlingly different face of the Long Island.

The east coast of Harris is a tumbled sea of rock, speckled with pocket handkerchiefs of green where crofters – who had been evicted from the fertile west to make way for the sheep flocks – once worked the inappropriately named lazy beds with the *cas-chrom*, a back-breaking foot plough.

At Tarbert, only a narrow isthmus of land keeps the Atlantic and the Minch apart. Twelve long Highland miles to the west and the imposing weather vane on the turreted tower of Amhuinnsuidhe Castle rears above a grassy bank. Below the road, the river foams down a narrow rock gulley; a spectacular sight when a midsummer flood brings the salmon leaping up the falls.

The public road is unique in the Highlands in that it commits *lèse-majesté* by abutting the frontage of the laird's Victorian mansion, Amhuinnsuidhe Castle. The house was a favourite retreat of Sir James Barrie, who frequently rented it in the summertime. It was here that Barrie wrote his famous play, '*Mary Rose.*'

The road ends at Hushinish, where the hills sweep down to the incomparable Hushinish Bay. By some mysterious alchemy of sea and fall of hill, the truly golden scimitar of sand at Hushinish has an ambience all its own. Unbeknowing, the American poet Stephen Vincent Benet spelled out the magic of the place in lines whose lingering cadence beats in time to the long, low rollers breaking slow on Hushinish Bay;

'This is where hiders live,
This is the tentative
And outcast corner where hiders steal away

To bake their hedgehogs in a lump of clay,
To raise their crops and children wild and shy
And let the world go by
In accidental marches of armed wrath
That stumble blindly past the buried path.'

The crofters of Lewis have a tenacious attachment to the sparse soil of their native island.

When the unco-operative natives compelled Lord Leverhulme to abandon his plans to revolutionize the fishing industry in Stornoway, the little Lancastrian switched his operations to Obbe on the Sound of Harris. The grateful burghers of long-neglected Obbe swiftly renamed the port Leverburgh in honour of their benefactor.

There was a brief blaze of prosperity, but on Leverhulme's death in 1925, the executors of his estate slammed down the shutters. Most of the costly installations were dismantled and sold as scrap. The Leverburgh boom perished in its infancy, although the name lives on. The ghost of Leverhulme haunts the place to this day, brooding over what might have been among the rusting industrial archaeology of the silent harbour.

The road west swings away from the bulging promontory of Toe Head – the lonely site of an ancient Celtic chapel – and follows the coast along the flowering machair fringing the

Above left. The shattered eastern seaboard of Benbecula merges into a spreading labyrinth of freshwater lochs. A dreary waste in the grey days of winter, summer can bring an almost incandescent quality of light so that the glowing browns of the moor and peat bogs seem to intensify the brilliant blues of the lochans.

Above right. On 29 August, 1930, St Kilda was evacuated at the request of the 26 islanders who remained. Now the military have moved in, and St Kilda has become a missile tracking base.

Left. The western sea breaks at Seilebost.

gleaming shell-sand beaches, passing Borve Lodge, the sheltered retreat of Leverhulme during his last days in Harris.

At the head of the Luskentyre estuary, a branch road runs along the foreshore to the village of Luskentyre under the lee of Ben Luskentyre. Something of the melancholy of the music of the west is reflected in the vast expanse of Traigh Luskentyre at full ebb, seen as the sun goes down over Taransay.

North Uist, Benbecula and South Uist are linked by causeways and bridges across the treacherous tidal sands of the old North Ford and South Ford. Although the traveller between the islands is no longer at the mercy of the tides, the sea remains the all-pervasive element in the Uists.

A nineteenth-century English traveller exclaimed in justifiable amazement, *'The sea here is all islands, and the land all lakes.'* It was an apt enough comment if lacking the poetic insight of the old Gaelic phrase, 'The Land below the waves.'

The shattered eastern seaboard, from the Sound of Berneray to the South Ford, merges imperceptibly into a spreading labyrinth of freshwater lochs. A dreary waste in the grey days of winter, but summer can bring an almost incandescent quality of light so that the glowing browns of the moor and peat bogs seem to intensify the brilliant blues of the lochans. No happier hunting ground for the angler exists.

South Uist is the complete antithesis of the urban ant-heap; tiny crofting townships dotted with white-walled, thatched cottages; black cattle grazing placidly on the fertile machair lands of the west coast; a life-style seemingly

139

Above left. A Carloway weaver at his loom.

Above right. A man and a small flock of sheep. Of little account in a table of computerized agricultural statistics, but an essential part of the fabric of island life.

Opposite. Casting a neighbourly eye.

immune to the frenetic pursuit of money.

But although Loch Bee is still a sanctuary for great herds of mute swans, the predilection of the military for the remote regions of the west has brought a rocket range to South Uist. The rocket range co-exists with the statue of Our Lady of the Isles on Reuval Hill, the snug cottages of Geirinish, true natives of the land under their thick cap of thatch, and the magnificent swans of Loch Bee; a trinity, it is devoutly to be wished, that will prove the more enduring.

Barra is the smallest of the Western Isles; the perfect miniature. To come to Barra from the south by light aircraft on a sunny day in early May is as exhilarating an experience as life has to offer.

In by Barra Head over the great cliffs of

Bernera, topped by the Barra Head Light 683 feet above high water. On over Barra's noble consorts – Mingulay, Pabay, Sandray, Vatersay – and rock-like Kisimul Castle guarding Castlebay. Dipping down over a jade-green sea broken by the glittering expanse of the Traigh Mhor; Ben Eoligarry thick with primroses; Atlantic rollers creaming on the white strand of the Traigh Uais; the sparkling cockle strand of the Traigh Mhor rushing up to meet the aircraft as it touches down on the shore.

In 1594, Dean Monro reported, *'This ile is full of grate cokills. Ther is na fairer sands for cokills in all the warld.'*

The great cockle strand has now become the fairest airport in all the world – and the only one to be under water twice a day.

ORKNEY

Only four districts in all Scotland produce more beef cattle than the expertly worked acres of the green isles of Orkney. Such stolid statistics, however worthy, quicken few heartbeats. But Orkney has much more to show than a century of progressive farming. Stone-Age man lived here, and his monuments have endured, giving another dimension to remote history.

Thousands of years after its completion, marauding Norsemen broke into the great burial cairn of Maeshowe in search of treasure. They left behind their runic graffiti, scratched on Maeshowe's ancient stones by swordpoint. Today, the Orcadian farmer's plough may skirt a prehistoric burial chamber, or turn up

Opposite. On the green island of Egilsay, the ruined Church of St Magnus, with its magnificent round tower miraculously intact.

Above. Kirkwall, fulcrum of the corporate life of the scattered islands of Orkney.

143

a stone axe-head, used perhaps in the building of the Ring of Brodgar, the Circle of the Sun.

On the green island of Egilsay the ruined Church of St Magnus – roofless, open to the sky, but with its magnificent round tower miraculously intact – marks one of the epic stories of the 'Orkneyinga Saga.'

In Holy Week in the year 1116, the cousins Magnus Erlendson and Hakon Paulson, joint inheritors of the Norse Earldom of Orkney came to the little island to settle their differences. Earl Magnus was the first to arrive. He spent the night in prayer in the church of the round tower. Earl Hakon came to Egilsay the following morning with an overwhelming force of war-galleys and warriors. The saintly Magnus offered himself for sacrifice to end the bitter factional strife that was wreaking havoc throughout the earldom.

To cynical twentieth-century eyes, Magnus may seem to have been avid for martyrdom. But this was the man who in earlier years had refused to take part in battle against the Welsh in the Menai Strait, saying, 'I have no quarrel with any man here.'

Magnus was slain by Earl Hakon's cook Lifolf after his standard-bearer Ofeig had rejected the role of executioner. The cook earned himself a baleful immortality in the Sagas.

The body of Earl Magnus was rowed over to Birsay and buried in the church his grandfather had founded. Before long, the people of Orkney were making pilgrimages to his grave, and miraculous cures were attributed to the saint.

Rognvald Kolson – poet, soldier, statesman, pilgrim to Jerusalem, and nephew of the martyred Magnus – vowed to build at Kirkwall a stone minster 'more magnificent than any other in these lands', in memory of his saintly uncle. In the year 1137, the first blocks of red and grey sandstone were laid, starting a work of centuries that was to become the cathedral church of St Magnus the Martyr.

St Magnus' Cathedral is the historic heart of Kirkwall, rising in splendour above the clustering grey-stone houses of the trim market town. Even the door of the cathedral has a nobility of scale in keeping with the grand design.

Kirkwall stands at the focal point of the islands on an isthmus where the east and west mainland meet, the fulcrum of the corporate life of the scattered islands of Orkney. Steamers nuzzle the pier, and a small boat crosses from Shapinsay with her daily complement of commuters.

Kirkwall's airport at Grimsetter stables a sturdy little work-horse of an aircraft, the *Islander*, which operates as an inter-island airbus. The *Islander* has transformed life for those in the distant North Isles.

The very first lighthouse in Orkney, at Dennis Head, North Ronaldsay, came into service in 1789, the year of the French Revolution. Nowadays, the keeper of the new light on North Ronaldsay can wait until he sees the *Islander* approaching before leaving for the landing strip and a quick trip to Kirkwall.

Island-hopping by air prints indelible images upon the retina of the mind; sun-basking

seals on a black reef at the tip of Stronsay, somnolent as the ghost village of Whitehall on the island, which once had 15 herring-curing stations served by 300 fishing boats working out of Stronsay; a line of brooding cormorants at Scabra Head, solemn as an assembly of kirk elders, guarding the approaches to Rousay; Noup Head Light on Westray, standing rock-fast on a great vertical bastion of cliff against an immensity of sea; creamy-green rollers breaking around Westray airstrip.

Coming in to North Ronaldsay by air is to have the fabric of a close-knit community un-ravelled before one's eyes. A six-feet high outer wall rings the island, excluding the native inhabitants – the famous wild sheep of North Ronaldsay – to the foreshore. Inside the circling wall, the trim chequerboard of intensively worked arable land becomes sud-denly magnified, exposing the Herculean labour that has gone into that cultivated land. The weathered roofs of houses loom into sharp focus, then the school, the church, the crowding headstones in the adjoining grave-yard – and all enclosed within that medieval fortress wall bounded by the sea.

The South Isles of Hoy – Haey, 'the high island', as the Norsemen knew it – Burray and South Ronaldsay form the enclosing arms of the anchorage of Scapa Flow, the major naval base of the Home Fleet in two world wars.

Scapa Flow was a prime target for German bombers and submarines in the Second World War. The first civilian in Great Britain to be killed in an air-raid by the *Luftwaffe* died in the little township of Bridge-of-Waithe. Ann

Opposite left. That sturdy little work-horse of an aircraft, the *Islander*, operates as an inter-island airbus.

Opposite right. It's roll-on, roll-off now at Scrabster and Stromness through the gaping jaws of the *St Ola*.

Above. This was the domestic life-style of the first Orcadians in the prehistoric village of Skara Brae, uncovered by a great storm in 1850.

Scott-Moncrieff's poem on how death came to Bridge-of-Waithe in the autumn of 1939 is an elegy distilled from the long history of Orkney where innocent lives so often came to a violent end by the capricious chance of a raiding party;

'. . . They were
Flying doon the twa lochs
Following the sheen o' the water
– Dost thoo mind? Ah, that time o' night –
And they winned at last to the brig,
Wide Waith that wreaths the salt tide wi'
  the fresh,
Whaur swan and eider sweem,
Whaur weed meets ware.
It's no a bonny place, nither here nor there,
Twa-three hooses and a dull-like shore . . .

Here John Isbister got his death,
Maggie o' Cumminness wi' many more
Fearful running to the door
Were stricken doon by door itsell,
Wall o' hoose, bombazement, shell,
The flying stove, the studdering road . . .'

At high tide on the night of 14 October 1939, a German U-boat squeezed a passage between Holm and Lamb Holm into the supposedly impregnable base of Scapa Flow. The *Royal Oak*, lying at anchor under the cliffs of Gaitnip, presented an easy target. The battleship was sent to the bottom, entombing more than 800 men.

The shock wave of the sinking in impregnable Scapa Flow triggered instant action. The eastern approaches to the Flow were sealed off by building causeways – the Churchill Barriers – between the islands of Lambs Holm, Glimps Holm, Burray and South Ronaldsay, all of which are now linked by road to the village of St Mary's on mainland Orkney.

Most of the work was done by Italian prisoners of war, who left behind their own Italian Chapel. This converted Nissen hut is a work of art; the delicate tracery of the wrought-iron screens a delight to the eye.

On the west mainland, the little town of Stromness (Hamnavoe, 'the haven inside the bay', of the Norsemen) clings to the crescent shore of its landlocked harbour under the lee of Brinkie's Brae.

Crow-stepped gable-ends meet like castle keeps above shoulder-width lanes sloping down to the harbour. Almost every house on the waterfront has its own pier or slipway, and

Opposite. Stromness, Hamnavoe of the Norsemen.

Above left. Even the door of St Magnus' Cathedral, viewed in isolation, has a nobility of scale in keeping with the grand design.

Above right. The Ring of Brodgar – the Circle of the Sun – overlord for countless centuries of the neck of land between the Lochs of Harray and Stenness.

every narrow close its beached boats. A stroll along the main street is a walk into the eighteenth century. The narrow, flagstoned street, with its thin cobbled centre strip for the vanished horse-drawn traffic, conveys a sense of community absent from the pallid urban stereotype instantly recognizable in town centres thoughout the land.

A prehistoric village, buried under sand for thousands of years, came to light when a great storm in 1850 uncovered part of the walls of Skara Brae. The stone huts of this small village on the edge of the sea, with their stone dressers, wall-cupboards, box-beds, passages and covered alleyways lifted long-closed shutters on the domestic life-style of the first Orcadians.

There is no aura of cosy domesticity about the Ring of Brodgar, the Circle of the Sun, overlord for countless centuries of the neck of land between the Lochs of Harray and Stenness. We owe the existence of the nearby Standing Stones of Stenness, the Temple of the Moon, to the protective zeal of a nineteenth-century historian, Malcolm Laing. He prevented the all too pragmatic tenant of Barnhouse Farm from breaking up the standing stones for use as a cow-byre.

Above. The sumptuous panache of the remains of Earl Patrick's Palace.

Opposite. A teeming tenement of kittiwakes near Marwick Head.

Orcadians are a pragmatic people. They are tough, undemonstrative, addicted to understatement. It is their great strength in the face of adversity or excessive good fortune. They need such qualities now as never before.

The tiny island of Flotta in Scapa Flow has become the giant oil terminal for pipelines pumping the black gold from deep-sea wells far from Orkney's shores. The flow of oil will not last forever. But neither did the dreadnoughts, which once lorded the waters of Scapa Flow, and Flotta survived their going. The folk of Flotta are better equipped than most for survival.

George Mackay Brown recounts the story of the two Flotta brothers who worked their croft together. Tiring of the work of the croft, one of them went off to Stromness, without a word to his brother, and enlisted in the Hudson Bay Company. He spent twelve years in Canada as a whaler and trapper, then took a passage home to Orkney.

His brother was sitting by the fire as he came into the croft house. Said the stay-at-home, *'Whare are thu been all this time?'*

Replied the wanderer, *'Oot.'*

SHETLAND

The definitive words on Shetland were written by the Roman historian Caius Cornelius Tacitus almost 2000 years ago. In clarity of expression and perceptive understanding, they have never been bettered; 'Nowhere,' wrote Tacitus, *'does the sea hold wider sway; it carries to and fro in its actions a maze of currents, and in its ebb and flow it is not held by the coast but penetrates deep into the land and winds about in the hills, as if in its own domain.'*

In Viking times, Shetland was the great sea cross-roads of the Norsemen on their voyages of discovery and conquest. The war-galley of King Haco, with its soaring, sumptuously gold-plated dragon's-head prow, was no stranger to Shetland.

Opposite. One of the natural treasures of Shetland, the bird cliffs of Hermaness.

Above. A familiar sight in Shetland waters.

151

The atmosphere in Shetland is still defiantly Norse, and the sea remains the dominant element in the life and work of Shetlanders. Rarely out of sight, poking restless, probing fingers into the innumerable voes and firths that cleave the coastline, the sea holds sway.

The riven rock-face of Eshaness, scourged by the relentless flail of the ocean, fights a losing battle against a sea hungry for further conquests as it comes roaring inland surging into the Holes of Scraada.

At no point in Shetland is the primacy of the sea more dramatically evident than Mavis Grind. The waters of Sullum Voe and St Magnus Bay threaten to overwhelm the frail neck of land exposed to the twin assaults of the North Sea and the Atlantic Ocean. The sea is supreme here; the land an insubstantial element, existing on sufferance.

Whether creaming over the black teeth of distant skerries, or lapping the sheltered green shores of tranquil voes, or washing Lerwick's crowded waterfront, the sea is the insistent interloper, never out of sight or mind.

Lerwick looks to the sea and lives from the sea. It is a fisherman's town, the narrow streets close-gathered to form a tight stockade against the weather. At the south end, tall houses rise out of the water rubbing shoulders with warehouses which harboured cargoes of contraband in the days when smuggling was an integral part of the Shetland way of life. Even today, their enclosed wharves have an aura of mystery, redolent of muffled oars, whispered commands, and midnight off-loadings on moonless nights.

Until 1712, when the imposition of the salt-duties crippled their enterprise, the rich Shetland fishings were the almost exclusive preserve of the Dutch. Upwards of 2000 round-bowed, broad-beamed, Dutch busses congregated in Lerwick harbour.

The teeming fishing grounds on the edge of the continental shelf near Shetland were known in the Netherlands as the 'Great Fishery', and the Dutch reaped a lucrative harvest for centuries. Shetland fishermen were in no position to compete, being shackled by their

own landlord-curers. The landlord-curers – and many of the merchants – operated an iniquitous truck system under which the fishermen were little better than serfs.

Working at a subsistence level, and chained by poverty to the 'sixerns' or six-oared open fishing boats, the men were at the mercy of the hazardous northern seas every time they left port. Those merciless seas exacted a cruel toll on their inadequate craft. On 20 July 1881, 10 sixerns foundered in a sudden gale, with the loss of 58 fishermen. Such disasters meant a collective death for those small townships of crofter-fishermen bereft of all their able-bodied men overnight.

A Royal Commission report led to the gradual ending of the truck system, and a fairer deal for the fishermen. The old open sixerns – lineal descendants of the Viking longship – were replaced with decked fishing boats able to operate at a much greater range from their home ports. A silver bounty of un-believable magnitude, in the shape of colossal shoals of herring, awaited them.

Opposite. Lerwick, the least parochial small town in Scotland, whose flagged streets are known to fishermen from every seafaring nation in Europe.

Above left. Lerwick is a fisherman's town, the narrow streets close-gathered to form a tight stockade against the weather.

Above right. Nowhere does the sea hold greater sway; it carries to and fro in its actions a maze of currents, and in its ebb and flow it is not held by the coast but penetrates deep into the land and winds about in the hills, as if in its own domain.

Opposite. Lerwick looks to the sea, and lives from the sea.

Above. Village settlements spanning 4000 years of human occupation have been painstakingly excavated at Jarlshof.

Left. Beached boats at the Bay of Spiggie on mainland Shetland.

In 1883, there were 807 boats fishing out of Shetland waters, landing their huge catches at 140 curing stations in the islands. The quantity of herring cured in that year reached the staggering total of 256,664 barrels.

Although the herring is no longer king, fishing remains a major Shetland industry. The enormous Baltic market for cured herring has gone, but shellfish are now exported direct from processing plants in Scalloway to Boston. Lerwick harbour, once the preserve of the sturdy Dutch fishing busses, now shelters a cosmopolitan fleet of Norwegian, Russian, Danish, Dutch, Polish, Icelandic and German fishing boats.

The waterfront encroaches upon the town. When the *St Clair*, the twice-weekly passenger and cargo steamer from Aberdeen, noses into her berth at the Victoria Pier, her bows soar high above the Market Cross, the hub of Lerwick. Ten streets and narrow closes radiate from the cross; an inviting labyrinth of meandering lanes reaching into the heart of the old town by paths denied to the ubiquitous car. Even the main street bears the splendid legend:

No cycling allowed in Commerical St.
Vehicular traffic not more than 4 m.p.h.

Lerwick is the least parochial small town in Scotland. Not many Londoners – or Glaswegians either, for that matter – can have walked the flagged close of Chromate Lane and observed the neat juxtaposition of the old and the new from the corner of Stout's Court. But these are familiar landmarks to fishermen from every seafaring nation in Europe.

Seen from the Scord of Scalloway, the ancient capital of Shetland nestles in a green hollow, shielded by Trondra Isle and the long, protruding neck of West Burra. With the sea creaming around Hoe Skerry, Papa Skerry and Green Holm; chestnut Shetland ponies grazing on the green pasturage of Berry Farm; great white galleons of cloud scudding across a thunderously Wagnerian sky – the Scalloway scene embodies the sense of space and gritty strength that is the essence of Shetland.

The spectacular ruin of Earl Patrick Stewart's castle broods over Scalloway's busy harbour where Shetland, Scottish east-coast, Norwegian and Dutch fishing boats berth amicably side by side. Earl Patrick's castle is a flamboyant reminder of the power that Shetland's warring earls once wielded. The piratical Earl Patrick press-ganged labour into the building of his castle, and local tradition

155

Above. Tall houses rise out of the water rubbing shoulders with warehouses which harboured cargoes of contraband in the days when smuggling was an integral part of the Shetland way of life.

Opposite. Keeping faithful watch over the sea, the indestructible Broch of Mousa.

maintains that the mortar was mixed with eggs and blood.

The island of Unst – claiming the most northerly house in the British Isles at Outer Skaw – attracts buyers from all over the world to its annual Shetland Pony Sales at Baltasound. Born to the freedom of the high scattald of Unst, many of the little Shetland colts and fillies are destined for the enclosed paddocks of the English Home Counties, whilst others are bound for an even stranger exile in America and Japan.

Saxavourd Hill affords a bird's-eye view of Muckle Flugga, Scotland's northernmost outpost and home of the Muckle Flugga Light. Rocky Muckle Flugga also houses a colony of thousands of swarming, argumentative gannets.

Baltasound has a little-known link with the English port of Bristol. Soapstone, used in the manufacture of roofing felt and ceramics, is quarried here. The sturdy little *Shetland Trader* operates a long-haul shuttle service to Bristol where the Unst soapstone is processed.

Fair Isle, that lonely stepping stone between Orkney and Shetland, is world famous as a staging post for migratory birds. Mariners have had less cause to bless its name. Many

vessels have met their end off its shores. In 1588, one of the ships of the Spanish Armada, the *El Gran Grifon*, commanded by Juan Gomes de Medina, was wrecked off Fair Isle. Of the 286 on board, 200 managed to struggle ashore. The survivors of that sixteenth-century wreck are reputed to have taught the women of Fair Isle the intricate knitwear patterns that are now synonomous with the island.

The bird observatory at North Haven is the best-known in Europe. Cedar-built, and superbly sited, the observatory has attracted not only ornithologists and naturalists to Fair Isle, but those eager to shed, if only for a week or two, the claustrophobic trappings of urban society. Simply to gaze out of the window of the common room is to experience a new world. The window looks out on the majestic Sheep Craig; a green-topped, horseshoe-shaped throne of stupendous proportions – a giant's throne, awaiting the coming of a Norse god.

The natural and man-made treasures of Shetland abound, open to all. There are the great bird-cliffs of Noss and Hermaness, justly rated – and not by ornithologists alone – as one of the wonders of the islands; and Fetlar can provide the rare sight of that natural aristocrat the snowy owl lording it over his new domain.

The excavations at Jarlshof have opened up the past, revealing village settlements spanning 4000 years of human occupation. And nowhere is that sense of the past stronger than in the ancient stones of the brave Broch of Mousa, still keeping faithful guard over Mousa Sound.

The old broch has witnessed the coming of many invaders, none stranger than the helmeted oil-men, ferried back and forth by helicopter between Sumburgh and their man-made islands of steel in the distant Shetland waters. Stranger still that they should have discovered the life-blood of industry below the sea-bed in such inhospitable seas so far from the great cities.

Paradoxes abound. Who would have thought that Sullum Voe – that long spear of the sea thrust deep into the gut of Shetland – would serve to guide oil pipelines to their landfall and become a terminal base known to oil-men the world over?

But when the last giant tanker has taken aboard the last cargo of oil at Sullum Voe, the Broch of Mousa will still be standing, and a new generation of Shetlanders will still be seeking to wrest a living from the cruel and bountiful sea.

157

Glenmore Forest Park 52
Glenshiel, battle of 76, 78
Golspie 96
Grant, Sir Ludovic 59–60
Grantown-on-Spey 59–60
Great Glen 45, 64
Grimsetter 144

Haco, King of Norway 120, 150
Hakon Paulson 144
Harris 130*, 132, 136–9
Helmsdale 100
Hermaness 150*, 157
Highland One 92*, 93
Holborn Head 112
Holes of Scraada 152
Holy Loch 24
Horlick, Sir James 13–15
Hoy 145
Hushinish 136–7

Innean a' Cheathaich 40
Inveraray 11*, 12–13, 21–2
Inverewe Gardens 85
Invergordon 91, 93
Inverness 63*, 64–6, 68–9, 70
Inverpolly Reserve 84
Invershin 105
Iona 36*, 37
Islay 15–16
Isle Ornsay 124
Italian Chapel 146

Jacobites 66, 73, 75–6, 78–9
Jarlshof 154*, 157
Johnson, Samuel 120, 122–7

Keith, George 73*, 75, 76
Kelvin, Lord 69, 93
Kilmun 24
Kinlochbervie 106–7
Kintail 72
Kintyre 7*, 8–13
Kirkwall 143*, 144
Kishorn 83
Kisimul Castle 141
Kyle of Lochalsh 120
Kyleakin 120
Kylerhea 120
Kylesku 107
Kyles of Bute 20

Lairg 96*, 101, 105
Lake Orcadie 117
Lazaretto Point 24
Lerwick 152*, 153*, 152–3, 155*, 155,
    156*
Leverburgh 137

Leverhulme, Lord 137
Lewis 132–6
Lews Castle 133
Lochs, Affric 62*
  Alsh 76, 79
  Awe 29, 30, 35*
  Bee 141
  Carron 79, 84*
  Cluanie 72
  Cuithir 127
  Eck 22
  Eil 48*, 49
  Etive 31, 32*
  Eunach 61
  Fyne 10*, 14*
  Garten 57
  Goil 21
  Gruinart 16
  Indaal 16
  Kishorn 76*, 76, 83
  Leven 44
  Linnhe 44, 47, 49
  Maree 74*, 83–4
  Morlich 52, 61
  Ness 69
  Scavaig 122
  Snizort 128
Lochaber 45, 46
Lochalsh 79
Lochcarron 80
Lochgoilhead 21
Lochindorb 60
Lorn 28
Lorn Furnacemen 28*, 30–1
Luskentyre 139
Lybster 116

MacDonald, Glencoe Massacre 40,
    42, 45
  of Sleat 120
  Sir Alexander 122
  Sir James 122, 124, 128*
Machrihanish 9
MacIan, 'The Old Fox' 42
Maeshowe 142
Magnus Barefoot 9
Magnus Erlendson,
    see Saint Magnus
Mallaig 45*, 48, 49
Mam Ratagan 85
Mary, Queen of Scots 97, 98
Mavis Grind 152
McAlpine, 'Concrete Bob' 48–9
  Malcolm 48–9
  Robert 48–9
McCaig, John Stuart 31–2, 35–6
Merry Men of Mey 115
Miller, Hugh 91, 120, 122

Minginish 120
Muckle Flugga 156
Mull 36–7
Murray of Atholl 25

Nature Parks, Reserves, Trails,
    Beinn Eighe 84
  Cairngorm 52
  Craigellachie 52
  Glenmore Forest 52
  Inverpolly 84
Needle Rock 127, 128*
Nelson, Lord 30–1
Nigg Bay 92*, 93
North Haven (Fair Isle) 157
North Ronaldsay 145
North Uist 139
Noss (Shetland) 157
Noss Head (Caithness) 112, 115*
Noup Head Light 145

Oban 27*, 31–2, 35–6
Obbe 137
Oil Industry, Ardyne 26
  Arnish Point 133
  Highland One 92*, 93
  Kishorn 83
  Nigg Bay 93
  Orkney 148
  Shetland 157
Old Man of Storr 125, 127
Ord of Caithness 112
Orkney 142–9
Osprey Hide, L. Garten 57, 59

Pabay 120, 122
Pass of Brander 30
Pentland Firth 115
Plockton 79–80, 85*
Pope, Alexander and the Reverend
    Alexander 116
Port Charlotte 14–15*, 15–16
Portree 125

Quiraing 125, 127
Queen Victoria 9, 42, 60

Raasay 125, 126*
Railways, Dingwall/Kyle of
    Lochalsh 93
  Fort William 47–8
  Fort William/Mallaig 48*, 48–9
  Inverness 68–9
  Oban 32, 35–6
  Wick/Thurso 112
Rannoch Moor 46*, 48
Reay 116
Reid Family 20